Evie Kemp

MUCH

A maximalist's guide to a creative home

KOA PRESS

@eviekemp

Con-
tents

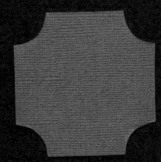

094
COLOUR +
PATTERN

124
LAYOUT +
LIGHTING

146
ART

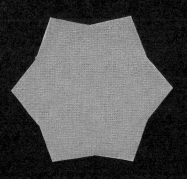

172
STYLING

196
SOURCING

216
MAKING

242
CELEBRATING

260
LAST BUT
NOT LEAST

270
THANK YOU

What's that
saying?
Go bold or
go home?
What if home
is bold?
Can I just...
stay home?

CHAPTER ONE

Intro

The hallway at my parents' house, hand-painted with stripes by my ever-creative mum, Angie.

I GREW UP IN A MAXIMALIST HOUSE, SO YOU COULD SAY I DON'T KNOW ANY BETTER.

When I was little, I had a recurring nightmare about being stuck behind the sofa cushions, unable to get out, with no one able to hear me scream. These days though, I'd be the first to dive headfirst into a pile of chintz pillows. What doesn't kill you makes you stronger.

I have lots of childhood memories of jumping across the living room floor because my mum was painting it; freezing winter mornings at car boot sales and local auctions looking for 'stuff'; running through the rain to rescue an old dining table from a skip; teaching myself about the intricacies of how a pattern repeats by sleeping under wallpapered ceilings (Laura Ashley of course); and watching my grandma create precision-made loose covers for all the family furniture, including my first sofa at age 17 – a grey and blue damask two-seater – I was a lot more cautious with my use of colour and pattern back then!

What you will find within this book is the story of my home – past and present. I am not an interior designer with a 'little black book' of A-List clients; I am a passionate creative usually working within a budget, finding joy and comfort through creating a home that reflects those that live in it. For me, that home consists of myself and my husband Sam, a doctor (by choice) and very talented (if reluctant) DIYer, and our pets – dogs Biggie and Pebbles and cats Maeby and Tweed.

Sam and I have been together since we were teenagers. He is my biggest supporter both emotionally and practically – you will see much of his DIY efforts in these pages – and while he still hasn't learnt to stop questioning some of my decisions (mostly the ones that require his expertise), he knows to say 'you were right' when they are done.

Growing Up

I was born in Sheffield, Yorkshire in the late eighties as the eldest of five siblings. At the time, my parents were both journalists working on local newspapers. When I was five, we moved a few hours south to Cambridgeshire so that my dad could study History at King's College, Cambridge as a mature student.

My parents purchased a dilapidated pair of workers' cottages in the village of Haddenham (in East Anglia) and knocked through the walls to make our family home. Almost everything was done by my parents on a tight budget but always in keeping with Mum's unique style. The kitchen benches were a patchwork of coloured tiles with curtained skirts; the pantry was a large old, free-standing cupboard with the previous owners' recipes still written on the inside of the door. My parents still have this in their home today, in New Zealand.

This was in the absolute heyday of Laura Ashley and our home was full of it. Think traditional floral prints in soft pastel colour palettes – a doll's house made big. The bedroom I shared with my younger sister, Gina, had blue and white ditsy-floral wallpaper. We were not allowed to stick posters over it, ever! The first poster I ever put on the wall was when I was 15. At the time I was outraged about not being allowed this simple form of self-expression; though now, after both paying for, and installing wallpaper myself, I get it!

Even with parental restrictions, I was very interested in making my space my own, and when inflatable furniture was a thing (I must have been about 10) I went all out. Somehow in our tiny bedroom I had a three-seater blow-up sofa in a black and white zebra print, with inflatable cushions and an inflatable footstool. Around the same time, I used vouchers I was given for Christmas to buy a karaoke machine the size of a bedside table (it was multi-purposed) and started undertaking some creative décor projects of my own. A memorable one was filling bottles with water and food colouring to make a rainbow. The blue one leaked, completely wrecking the top of my pine chest of drawers … eat your heart out Laura Ashley!

While space was somewhat tight upstairs with seven of us living there, we had a snug, separate little cosy room almost exclusively used in the evenings, and for watching television. As a primary-schooler my favourite TV show was *Antiques Roadshow*, and any kind of home or design makeover show. *Changing Rooms* was an obvious hit and honestly, I still have a soft spot for Laurence Llewelyn-Bowen, though perhaps now my admiration is more for his unerring confidence and self-assuredness in the face of truly awful ideas.

My mum, Angie, loved (and still does) a 'Changing Rooms' moment, and if ever one of us was away – at camp, or staying with our grandparents – we would inevitably come home to a bit of a makeover. I remember coming home once to find the floorboards in my bedroom newly painted in a light blue wash to match the wallpaper – I was delighted.

While a lot of the time my childhood was pretty low-key, if a bit quirky, my dad's affiliation with King's College meant some grand and privileged experiences. Mum would take us into the university museums where we were often the only visitors, to sketch from Charles Darwin's animal specimens. We also got invited to the King's College Children's Christmas party, and despite it being the fanciest

I have lots
of childhood
memories of
jumping across the
living room floor
because my mum
was painting it.

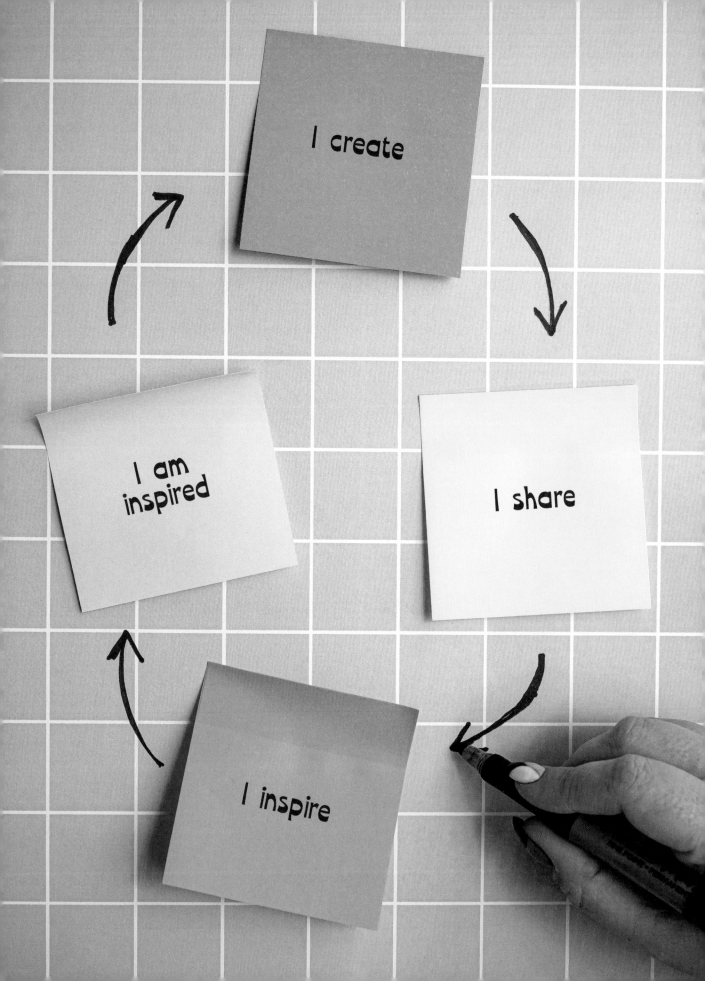

Christmas party for children, it was not one we got excited about. While Father Christmas would be there, the gifts were often historical and academic in nature (jigsaws of British kings and queens and so forth), and the other children were intimidatingly posh – in my mind anyway.

I tend to talk about my mum a lot when it comes to home, but I do have a wonderful dad, Geoff. One who mostly has his head in a book but who is always prepared to talk passionately about art, books, and books about art. I have never met a more prolific reader than my dad, and if he had his way when it came to interior design, every wall would be lined with bookshelves.

When my dad received his doctorate and a teaching position in New Zealand in 2001, family life changed dramatically.

House hunting with my parents was a thrill for me at age 14, and ultimately fuelled a lifelong obsession for finding my friends and family the perfect home! On arrival in New Zealand my parents fell in love with Devonport, a pretty Auckland suburb filled with heritage wooden villas, painted white with picket fences and grand old trees in their front gardens. Entirely over budget for a new academic and his large family of two adults and five kids! Luck was on their side however and a place was available in the old Devonport Power Station – a Victorian brick building divided into three units. As soon as we walked in, I was obsessed. At that point I had lived

my whole life in a small village in extremely 'normal' style houses and brick bungalows. Here, I was walking into a TV show.

It is a hard place to describe – set across four floors, with eighties-style industrial handrails on the stairs and double-height ceilings in the open-plan living space. It was quirky and odd, and I know my parents will say it had more than a few issues, but to me it was a New York loft.

I have stayed in Auckland ever since, though moving around various suburbs, flats and apartments. After leaving school I embarked on studying Law and History of Art at university, where I struggled with depression and anxiety. At 19 I dropped out of university and barely left my room for months. As I sought the help I needed and started to feel better, I focused on what I really wanted to do with my life; what I could do that would help me be happier.

I decided to apply for graphic design. I had been deterred from studying art by a harsh secondary-school teacher, so with no school work to submit I put together a portfolio from scratch and sent in my applications. I scraped in at the last minute, after being waitlisted to study at the Auckland University of Technology (AUT), and I nervously started the semester unsure of what to expect.

I'm still not entirely sure what led me to study graphic design. I imagined I would work on newspapers and magazines, and I did for a while after graduating, but I was really lacking in

Opposite: During Lockdown I painted the back of this built-in bookshelf to better display some of my favourite things. Page 24: This pink dog painting by UK artist John Bond was one of the first original pieces of art I ever bought and has lived in many parts of the house. Here it is on an art deco table painted in glossy sky blue that I bought via Instagram. Page 25: For several years the POP! prints in the entranceway welcomed guests and really set a tone for what to expect from our home.

confidence when it came to my creativity and artistic ability. I knew I had to do something creative but wanted a 'safe' path, with rules to learn and skills to master. Basically, I had very little idea of what graphic design really was.

While at design school we learnt all sorts of different disciplines: life drawing, photoshop, dry-point etching, packaging design ... but it was illustration that really caught my imagination. I had two great illustration tutors, Chris Mousdale and Simon Clarke, who encouraged and inspired me to find my own style. Under their guidance I found my passion. I took evening classes to learn how to create repeating patterns, as at that time there wasn't a textile-design paper, and learned how to digitally print fabric – extremely slowly. My final exhibition project culminated in a garish and aggressive range of fabrics that I applied to furniture and lampshades. Pieces I still have in my home today.

In my final year of my graphic design degree, I started to share pictures of my work (and my dogs) on a new app called Instagram. I created art prints of my animal illustrations and sold them at craft markets and eventually online. I shared images of my home as I styled my prints for sale, and that, I suppose, was the starting point of everything I do

today in art, craft and interiors. I create, I share, I inspire, I am inspired, I create.

Growing up, and still today, I am inspired and influenced by talented, generous and creative women. As I look around my home now, I see the colour they have brought to my life. Throughout this book I will reference these special people and the experiences that shaped me.

Our homes should be full of stories. I know mine isn't complete without them. I hope as you read through this book you think about the people, and the experiences that make up who you are. That you gain the confidence and skills to be able to communicate that through your home.

These days, you will mostly find me on Instagram where there is a fabulous and ever-growing community of maximalists, artists, designers and other creatives that embolden and inspire me. I really recommend finding your people (and me! @Eviekemp) on there so we can cheerlead you on as you embark on your own colourful world journey.

Evie x

I've always been inspired and influenced by talented, generous and creative women. As I look around my home now, I see the colour they have brought to my life.

CHAPTER TWO

Story-telling

I have a penchant for giant and tiny things and both the badminton racquet and banana cushion were 'must-haves'; the David Shrigley tea towel (framed on the wall) says it all.

MAXIMALISTS ARE BORN, NOT MADE.

But as we grow up, we are constantly fed messages on toning it down and not standing out. I have already talked about the seeds of creativity and experiences I had when I was young, but honestly, I became a teenager and just kind of erased that all from my brain. I wanted to be cool and I was far more interested in hanging out with my friends than looking at art.

As we get a bit older, we often find ourselves being moulded again – into what we think we should be. Forget the zebra-print inflatable sofa, you're an adult now – what do adults like?

Over time, societal expectations dampen us down and make us afraid and untrusting of our own mind; it's almost exactly the same as that point growing up where you feel you *must* fit in. And what does growing up look like? Weirdly, it seems to look like a flat-pack laminate TV cabinet and a grey couch.

I want you to fight it. The world doesn't get to decide what you like. *You* get to decide.

I won't go into a full rant about capitalism, but who really stands to gain from trends and having everyone thinking they must all buy the same things? Why is success defined as a new SUV or a fridge with an icemaker (this is a bit of a sore point actually, because we just bought a fridge without one and I miss it)? How is having a beautiful home dependent on having giant windows and a marble bench?

Why is it not having a space that feels safe and joyful and welcoming? It can all get a bit depressing – okay, *very* depressing. But we're not here to get angry about that stuff. Well, maybe just a little bit … passion is good!

It is absolutely freeing to discover your own style. The personal trends within that stuff that you actually really like – not just what shops you want to buy from – and using that stuff to create a home you will love forever. It will bring a confidence that extends into all facets of your life.

Since you're reading this, I'm going to guess you already have the itch to bring a little maximalism into your life; a touch of pattern here and there perhaps. Or if you're like me, a riot of texture, personality, pattern clashing. A home drenched in colour.

This book, in part, is a practical guide to designing with maximalism, as well as a source of inspiration, but above all I hope it gives you the permission you need to fill your life with colour and pattern and to find the things you love, and enjoy them to the fullest.

Because once you embrace always being 'too much', that's where the magic really happens. It's a lot of not caring what other people think, but caring an awful lot about yourself.

Ready? Of course you are.

You Don't Need a Label, it's a Spectrum
Like minimalism, maximalism exists in all art forms and while in many ways complete opposites, minimalism and maximalism actually have a fair bit in common. They are both styles concerned with the impact of our surroundings and the presence or absence of 'stuff' on our wellbeing.

Minimalism has gained a lot more positive press in recent decades, so in some ways it seems more socially acceptable. But maximalism has always been there, doing its thing, collecting vases and cushions and awaiting its day in the sun.

The world has changed dramatically over the last few years with the pandemic and our focus was turned towards home. For a couple of years, we had nowhere else to go, and so for many, 'home' has done some serious overtime. It has provided the necessities, but also had to keep our spirits up, inspire us, delight us, make us laugh, and most importantly make us feel safe. And while for many of us, life has returned somewhat to normal, we have a new realisation of how fragile the world is, and how important it is to influence the part of it that we belong to.

A Short History
Maximalism is described as the aesthetic of excess, but that doesn't mean hoarding piles of old tat. The key is in the word aesthetic; maximalism comes in many styles but it is always carefully collected and curated. Certain styles and design movements naturally lend themselves more easily to maximalism – boho, retro, art deco, Arts and Crafts to name a few. Whereas more modern design movements such as Scandi and modernism are instantly aligned with minimalism.

We see maximalism expressed in many different eras of history; it adapts and evolves to fit times and taste. Perhaps the most recognisable maximalists would be the Victorians – they loved stuff. They were avid collectors, and advances in transportation, trade and industry meant they had a lot to show off. Interiors were dense with texture, colour and pattern; reflecting a fascination with the exotic and the technological advancements of the time, like gas lighting, which allowed for more detailed and vibrant interior decorations. They loved richly patterned wallpapers, deeply dyed fabrics, exotic palms, heavy, elaborately carved furniture, and knick-knacks. Lots of knick-knacks.

As we stepped into the 20th century, art nouveau popped up with its own twist on maximalism. It was

We see maximalism expressed in many different eras of history; it adapts and evolves to fit times and taste.

Once you embrace always being 'too much', that's where the magic really happens.

Give space to what really matters to *you*. Remember, this is your home, feather your nest.

all about smooth lines, nature-inspired patterns, and making everyday objects look like pieces of art. This movement really wanted to mix what we thought of as 'real' art with the stuff we use every day, leading to some incredible interiors decked out with custom-made furniture, stained glass, and fabrics that gave a nod to the natural world.

Alongside this we had (my personal favourite design era) the Arts and Crafts Movement, hitting back at the cold, mass-produced vibe of the industrial age. It was all about the charm of something made by hand, bringing warmth and personality straight into the home. Think cosy spaces filled with wooden touches, natural colours, and William Morris's patterns inspired by the great outdoors. This movement made every piece feel special, like it had a story to tell – maximalism with a heart. It showed us the beauty of filling our spaces with things that mean something; setting the scene for how we personalise our homes today.

Then came art deco, riding the wave of the roaring twenties. It sharpened up maximalism with

neat, symmetrical designs, and wasn't shy about using flashy materials like gold, silver, and all sorts of fancy woods. This era was all about luxury, showing off, and embracing the good life, with interior design that shouted, 'look at me' and celebrated being bold and forward-thinking.

Jumping through the mid-century and swinging into the seventies, maximalism took on a whole new vibe. The mid-century brought us pops of bold colours and fun, experimental shapes that played with the traditional notions of space and form. Then, as the seventies rolled in, it cranked up the volume even more: psychedelic patterns, a kaleidoscope of colours, and a mix of textures that could make any room feel like a party. This era embraced a more-is-more attitude, ditching the restrained for the expressive. It was all about creating spaces that were not just lived in but were *felt*; every piece told a story and rooms weren't just rooms, but experiences.

We continue to see the influence of all these previous incarnations of maximalism in how we design our homes today. The bulbous, curvy and super comfortable furniture shapes of the 1970s, the Victorian popularity of decadent wallpaper, the Arts and Crafts passion for natural materials and honest design are all things we see strongly appearing in contemporary interiors today.

They do say there is nothing new in this world, which is somewhat true – but how we put objects and designs together has an infinite number of possibilities and this is where you (or I) come in.

The beauty of maximalism is that you don't need to adhere to just one, or in fact *any* particular style or era. You create your own style symphony, and the rich layers and juxtapositions mean every single maximalist creates in their own completely unique way.

Previous: The lounge has changed many times over the years. The orangey-red walls were a bold move, even for me, but a wonderful colour to experiment with. Especially when it came to layering textiles. Opposite: I play around with style a lot depending on where my interests are currently focused. Here the snug was very much influenced by British interiors and colours and fabrics in a more Arts and Crafts style.

And, not to throw shade, ahem, but I don't think minimalists are afforded that kind of scope!

I'm still not able to put a label on my own style, and this used to trouble me – thinking it meant I didn't have a style. But I am at peace with it now, because *I* know what I like, and what I don't. I know that my own style comes from various eras, styles and design movements. How I mash it all together is my secret sauce. Just as your own recipe will be unique to you. By living this way it's near impossible that any of us could be the same. Not something you'd think walking into most furniture stores – who want us all to like exactly the same thing this season, and then hate it the next.

I'd be lying if I said I wasn't influenced by trends – I'm human after all and I love design so of course I'm constantly intrigued and interested, but I know now how to tell if I really like a trend or if I'm just being carried away on the tide. I'm also aware of how likely I am to still like an on-trend item years later and how heavily to invest. Usually I will just add in a little bit of that thing, rather than redesign the whole house, but I'll never say never!

Being Brave

Part of what makes maximalism brave is that through it we share our souls. I want to see the life you lead reflected in your interiors – or, the life you *want* to lead. Have you ever heard the term 'speak it into existence'? Well, we're going to *style* it into existence. Create the space in your home to house the person you want to be.

You don't have to have your home the way anyone else does. My dining room is now an art studio, and my sitting room is now my wardrobe. Ta da – the uninspired me is now a fashionable and artistic me. What was the dining room doing for me anyway?

You don't have to have extra rooms and great cavernous spaces to live a life on your own terms. Do you need an office? Create one in the cupboard that is currently holding your old clothes, or in the corner of your lounge. Where in your home do you spend all your time? Is your bedroom a suntrap while your lounge is freezing? Maybe your bedroom needs a beautiful armchair that you can read in, to make the most of the sunshine.

If you are an avid cook, instead of a streamlined kitchen maybe you'd like a massive free-standing pantry and a storage-filled buffet in your dining space. Give space to what really matters to *you*. Remember, this is your home, feather your nest.

The benefits to sharing so much of ourselves are twofold – we give ourselves permission to be who we really are, and by extension we let others in. It can be scary to start with, but I promise it's worth it. I think most of us have felt that anxiety ... of being judged on the way our home looks. But if you like your visitors enough to let them in the door, then you should be happy for them to learn a little about you from the story being told by your interiors.

I'm aware that I give the impression of always being comfortable in my own skin and unafraid to stand out, and honestly? That still surprises me. Because in reality I was a late bloomer, and I'll probably be blooming until the end. I have experienced the weight of others' expectations (real and imagined), I have been bullied for being

Create the
space in
your home
to house the
person you
want to be.

Home for me must be comfortable as well as beautiful. I'm not ever looking for perfection, just somewhere lovely to curl up with a book and my pups.

different, and then done everything in my power to attract as little attention as possible.

Like many women, my body has been a source of great shame ever since I can remember. Most of my twenties were spent covering up every part of me and really living in a state of self-loathing. I felt like my body was betraying my main goal in life – to not be noticed. At the same time, working on my art and embracing my love of interiors became a real outlet for me. Somewhere along the line, as I started getting braver with what I was doing, my self-confidence grew. I knew more about myself, and I was surrounding myself with things that mattered to me. I don't know if it's this that made me realise I mattered too or just that life is too short to restrict yourself from a full and happy life, but my creativity stretched over into my personal style and how I approach my whole life. The more it did, the happier I was.

My body hasn't changed, but my mind has.

Honestly, I could write a whole book on body acceptance – and while this isn't it, I think it's worth thinking about what you're giving your energy, mind space and even happiness to. What myths have you believing you're not worth exploring, expressing and celebrating? If you're addicted to blending in, how has this made you feel safe?

Just like the saying 'Dress for the body you have now', I'd say 'Design for the home you have now'. You don't need to wait until you get your own place, or buy your first home, or build your dream home. If we're always looking to tomorrow, what is making today special?

Unlocking Your Story

Good design in any form should tell a story, but maximalism is a whole omnibus. It has chapters, developed characters and history, as well as an endless potential for change. It has a richness that can't be bought from a shop or replicated in another home because each element and object brings its own story, which combined with the others, makes a new one.

Often seeing your own story is the hardest part; it can feel a bit like talking about yourself for too long at a dinner party – self-indulgent and vain. But this is your home, and your life, and so who cares if your bedroom is completely over-the-top you?

The truth is, as humans we love to know what makes each other, well, human. While it's unavoidable that your home will say a lot more about you once you embrace this, accept that it is a wonderful tool for connection. Letting people in (literally) can really mean letting people in (metaphorically). People will feel the story you're telling them when they enter your home. It's powerful and inspirational, it should make you feel cocooned and loved, and make others intrigued, beguiled and completely enchanted.

Is there a home you have been to that has made you feel these things? Somewhere that you thought was just lovely. What made it so? It might be a friend, neighbour or family member's home – or even just a home you visited. It often won't even be a home that is to your own style, but one that expresses so perfectly the unique lives that play out within it.

Just like the saying 'Dress for the body you have now', I'd say 'Design for the home you have now'.

You know that feeling when you have caught sight of a bookshelf loaded with great books and you can't stop scanning the spines even though you feel a bit nosy? You feel inspired to read and take mental notes for books to borrow. It makes you think of your own favourite books, and it tells you so much about the person who has amassed this collection. This is exactly what we're doing, but in a way that extends far beyond the bookshelf. Your story is yours to craft and yours to enjoy, but it also feels wonderful to see others enjoy it too.

Having a home that tells a story, isn't about giving away your entire life story with clues scattered around the house as if Sherlock Holmes might pop by (I wish). Rather, it's that by having items you love, and not denying things that might seem out of place or a bit cheesy or sentimental, your home will beautifully and simply tell the tale of who lives there.

Even the most minimal or seemingly impersonal home contains items that speak to who lives there, and as you embrace them you'll bring in more.

Remember, you will always be the most interesting thing in your home!

My mother-in-law Lea's home is one so rich in stories. It really is a home that befits its owner, for Lea has spent a lifetime travelling the world and pursuing her studies in spirituality (I am painting with a broad brush here as she has such wide-ranging knowledge and interests). She collects items from every place she visits – things that mean something to her and that will intentionally remind her of a place, a time or an experience – and her house is full of them. Books,

art, sculptures, ceramics, textiles – nothing in Lea's house is without a story or meaning; nothing is there 'just because'.

The joy and peace that home brings to Lea is palpable; it is her retreat, her haven and her place to recharge. We recently helped her move house, a process that was extended somewhat by the stories that came out of each and every box (and there were many!). But what a wonderful and inspiring way to be. We might not all be at Lea's level of storytelling just yet (and possibly never, let's be honest), but there are so many ways we can bring these parts of ourselves into our homes.

If you're feeling really stuck on seeing your story ... Take inspiration from the prompts to the right. Let them remind you that you are a complete and wonderful human being with a lot to share and celebrate. Be proud of your interests and allow yourself to indulge them a little. Remember they don't need to be grand. What makes us interesting is that we're all different. That's grand in itself.

When you have completed your list, in the second column brainstorm the ways you might visually share these things. For example, perhaps you really love musicals. Could you collect some old record covers or playbills to frame? Or sheet music? Is there something in a character or a set that inspires your own home? A secret (or not so) nod to something that makes you happy. A special something you'd love to collect but have never seen the point. The point is, it makes you happy – that is enough.

Favourite ...	Decorating ideas
Things to do	
Things to watch/read what eras are you drawn to in movies or novels?	
Food to cook/eat	
Items to wear	
People to see	
Places to go	

The green ceramic poodle was a gift from my mother-in-law Martine from France, the eye artwork was given to me by my friend, artist Fleur Woods, and the Japanese-style lady is an old 'paint by numbers' artwork from the 1960s I found in an antique shop in Taranaki.

STORY STARTERS

While I believe almost anything can tell a story, here are a few solid ideas to get your story started and how to get your home speaking to you.

1 Books

Books are an obvious place to start; our bookshelves speak volumes (excuse the pun) about us and we can use them to say even more. For example: you're a real foodie and you love cooking and entertaining – instead of keeping your favourite, beautiful recipe books on the kitchen shelf, use a couple stacked on the bench, with a dish loaded with the seasonal vegetables you've bought that week.

For a friend of mine who is a clothes stylist, we picked out her fashion books and styled them with her most extravagant pair of sunglasses on top as part of her office décor. I like to pick up old books just for the spines and covers and often they're things that make me laugh more than anything else. One of my favourites, that I always have on display, is a book titled *Eating People is Wrong*. Hopefully it says more about my dark sense of humour rather than that I am a recovering cannibal – but honestly, either is interesting!

2 Textiles

Fabric patterns originate from all over the world and from all periods in time. They also appear in items that often travel through lives – quilts, clothing, rugs and furniture – either down through generations or across seas as they're easily folded and stored (and too often forgotten). Perhaps you have fabrics that tie to your own personal heritage, or that remind you of places you have travelled to? Maybe you have seen a pattern that takes you back to your childhood, or perhaps it's just something you really love and it makes you happy. These are all valid reasons to include a fabric in your décor. And arguably more valid than 'it matches'.

When we look at the history of rugs and carpets from different parts of the world, many of them are telling a story through actual figurative narrative, the history of the technique and materials as well as the hidden symbols and motifs in patterns. We might not be weaving our own rugs now (I take my hat off to you if you are) but we can collect and use textiles that connect with us in some way beyond being purely practical.

3 Heirlooms

By heirlooms I mostly mean pieces that have been passed on through the family that often are more sentimental than valuable. These objects, while mostly loved, are often the cause of frustration – shoved in a corner or stuffed in a cupboard because we don't know 'how' to incorporate them into a modern home. Generally, the only thing making these objects feel awkward is our own lack of confidence in how to use them, but it really is as simple as acknowledging 'this is something important to me and I like having it in my home'.

Displaying these items proudly instantly makes a unique design statement and you will find your mindset reframing from 'How do I make this fit?' to 'What else fits?'.

I once styled a house with very few personal objects in it, but tucked away was an amber-coloured 1970s 'genie bottle' that had belonged to my client's grandmother. I used that as the starting point for the whole lounge redesign. When she saw it, she said the old bottle was the best part of the transformation because now she could truly enjoy it.

An artwork by my friend Fleur Woods

I made this Pojagi, which is a Korean method of quilting with two sides to allow the light to shine through

Sculptures by artist Selwyn Muru – he was our neighbour when I was a teenager and gifted these to my parents

This is the TV (shhh) ↗

Painted cabinet I brought home from a magazine shoot. I'd painted the doors closed (since rectified)

Mixing textiles – old/new, high end/high street

I persuaded my mum to buy this Sighthound sculpture at a market about 20 years ago. She gave it to me recently

LOVE

The Life Eclectic
RAE MORRIS

This Ikea bookshelf on its side is the perfect home for some of my pottery collection

When I bought this sofa for $100 we couldn't fit it in the house so my friend stored it until we moved

A Note About 'Special Things'

Remember that today is a special day, as is tomorrow, as is the next day, as is Wednesday 17 weeks from now. Even (or especially) our most precious items deserve to be seen, used and enjoyed as much as possible. Keeping a special tea set covered in dust unseen for 50 years is a waste. Displaying it (safely) and using it occasionally will only make it more special. Yes, accidents may happen, but they might happen even when something is tucked in the back of the cupboard. Just as these treasures are a part of our own story, we are a part of theirs. So use these things, make the memories, and most of all, enjoy them.

✳

If it's something you really can't bear to risk damaging, consider alternative ways you can help preserve it where it can still be enjoyed. For example, box frames, or glass-front cabinets; using museum wax to hold items in place, or repurposing, such as taking a fragile textile and carefully making it into a lampshade that can be used for many, many years to come.

Remember, you will always be the most interesting thing in your home!

CHAPTER THREE

Finding your own style

While my style has changed, lots of pieces stay,
though styled in different ways. These little resin
budgies by Pete Cromer will always be watching over
the front door. Next left: My dressing room is a place
just for fun and somewhere I want to be able to see
everything. I turned the cupboard into a boot display
using Ikea drawers at the bottom and shelves above.

I WILL BE REALLY HONEST HERE: I FEEL LIKE I'M STILL FINDING MY OWN STYLE, AND I THINK I ALWAYS WILL BE.

t's what I love most about design – it's constantly evolving and changing as I myself change. I feel like I'm forever finding what works for me and honing in on that. As my taste, trends and needs change, so does my style. But – the freedom and confidence I move my style around with is underpinned by having my own base style as a foundation to extend upon.

The single biggest piece of advice I can give to unleashing your style is just that – unleash! Stop restricting yourself and stop second-guessing yourself. If you really love something, be it a wallpaper, a colour, a 10-foot pink giraffe – make it happen.

If you love everything you have chosen then they will work together because they are linked by you.

Which not only is a great enabler for buying that thing you have had your eye on, but a real confidence builder. If you're choosing objects purely on if they 'go' with other objects, you're going to get further and further removed from what really lights you up.

Your aim in every single room is to be able to look at anything and think 'Gosh I love that coaster/ lamp/cushion/whatever'. This process involves a bit of indulgence and taking the job of curation seriously. For example, you might have a lamp but you don't love it; instead, you really want a lamp you have seen at auction. Rather than thinking 'I already have a lamp, I don't need it', consider beyond the practical, about how it will make your home, and by

The single biggest piece of advice I can give to unleashing your style is just that – unleash!

Clockwise from left: Before this round brick room became my dressing room it was a small sitting room, we actually already had the curved pink settee from our last house – getting it in, and then out, of the doorway was a challenge!; while the marble table is mostly immovable, I change this dining space around by switching out the lampshade, artwork and seat pads on the dining chairs. I also paint this wall quite often (it may be mostly paint at this point); a butter dish by artist Sophia Holt; a retro West German vase.

extension, you, feel. Buy the lamp if you can, and sell, donate, rehome or reuse the old one.

It might sound or feel indulgent or even wasteful at first, but it is far from it – it's becoming mindful about what you consume and purchasing items that nurture as well as function, that will be treasured for many years. Wherever possible I shop second-hand and get an added thrill from giving something a new life.

It has been many years since I have bought something on a whim, only to want to replace it the next month or year, as increasingly everything has both function and beauty (in my eyes)! Right down to the littlest things – we keep our toothpaste standing up in a little claw-foot ceramic vase that I've had forever. I like it and it makes me happy; it's my style and I know it.

You won't be replacing everything in your home every week; it's a gradual process because we are creating a home for life, not for a season.

You will know you have your style pegged when you're confident and happy in your choices from toilet roll holders to a full dining suite.

STYLE BASICS

If we break it down, there are a few main elements of your own style which you need to figure out to create a complete picture of your style. You will already know your own style influences, eras of inspiration, and be able to recognise designers and décor you love (refer to your favourite things list if you need a prompt, page 043), but it might all be a bit hidden under years of liking what you've been told to like. It's that box at the back of the garage packed full of things you loved so much but have long forgotten was even there. Let's unpack that!

1 Colour Palette

Finding your way with colour is the biggest key to unlocking and understanding your style. The way we each use colour is incredibly personal. We'll talk about colour in more detail soon (See Chapter Five).

2 Eras and Designs

Eras and styles of furniture, art and objects you like – this will be a combination of things. You don't need to think about how you're going to put that hand-carved Balinese cabinet with a chintz

You will know you have your style pegged when you're confident and happy in your choices from toilet roll holders to a full dining suite.

As a solution to our boring bathroom tiles, I created a 3D mural by cutting shapes out of MDF, painting them and attaching them to the tiles using adhesive Velcro.

armchair and graphic wall mural (um, sounds amazing) just yet. Just write down the design items and influences that really get you excited (these can be items you own and items you wish you did!).

3 Art

We're all drawn to different styles of art, especially when it comes to art we have at home. What would be your dream pieces? Do you love some bright, bold pop art? Or an atmospheric landscape painting? Perhaps, an eclectic mix of mid-century portraits? Or some slick black and white photographic works?

4 Min/Max

Where do you fall on the maximalist/ minimalist scale? How full do you like your home to feel? This can grow over time as it takes some getting used to, to figure how maximalist you really are.

If you are still feeling a little unsteady about where to start to flesh out your own style …

WORKPAGE – FINDING YOUR STYLE

Look around your home for commonalities – what do you see repeated: colours, metallics, stripes, cushy furniture, plants, natural elements?

* Name two TV programmes you love for their aesthetic – think about their interiors, where/when are they set? What do you love about the vibe?

* What colours and style do you like to wear? What fabrics are you drawn to? What types of patterns?

* Think back on your childhood home or a special place that you have lived – what's one thing in that home that comes to mind as something you loved?

* When you visit other homes what is it that you find yourself drawn to? Is it homes with big kitchens, a tiny house with a rambling garden, a luxurious bedroom?

* I'm going to use myself as an example here to come up with a list of terms and styles that are relevant to me and then I'd love for you to do the same. Start by looking around your own home, and then move on to magazines and online. If you're unsure of what style or era something is from, save the picture and search by image on Google – looking out for keywords that appear on similar pieces – a little bit of detective work.

* All of these aspects will probably shift and change over time. Trust those shifts as proof of your own style rather than doubt that you have any! …

Colour Palette
✳ I love colour, especially pinks, reds and oranges.
✳ I like mid-tone colours that are slightly 'greyed off' or chalky in tone.
✳ I enjoy punchy colour combinations.

Eras and Design
✳ I love 1970s-style upholstered furniture with low seats and lots of curved lines.
✳ I like shiny surfaces of glass, chrome and stone.
✳ East Asian-style furniture, ceramics and art are something I'm drawn to.
✳ I'm also heavily influenced by the Bloomsbury Group and Arts and Crafts era.

Art
✳ I mostly like figurative art (portraits, still lifes, interior scenes) but I'm pretty open-minded and just enjoy art in general.
✳ I also like a lot of contemporary and especially sculptural pieces.

Min/Max
✳ I REALLY like cushions and I really like having lots of art on the wall.
✳ But, I also like having some more ordered areas, and some bare surfaces.
✳ It is important to me that a space is easy to move through and around.

THE FUTURISTIC PARADE

"The Damsel of Coucy"   "...Champs Elysées"

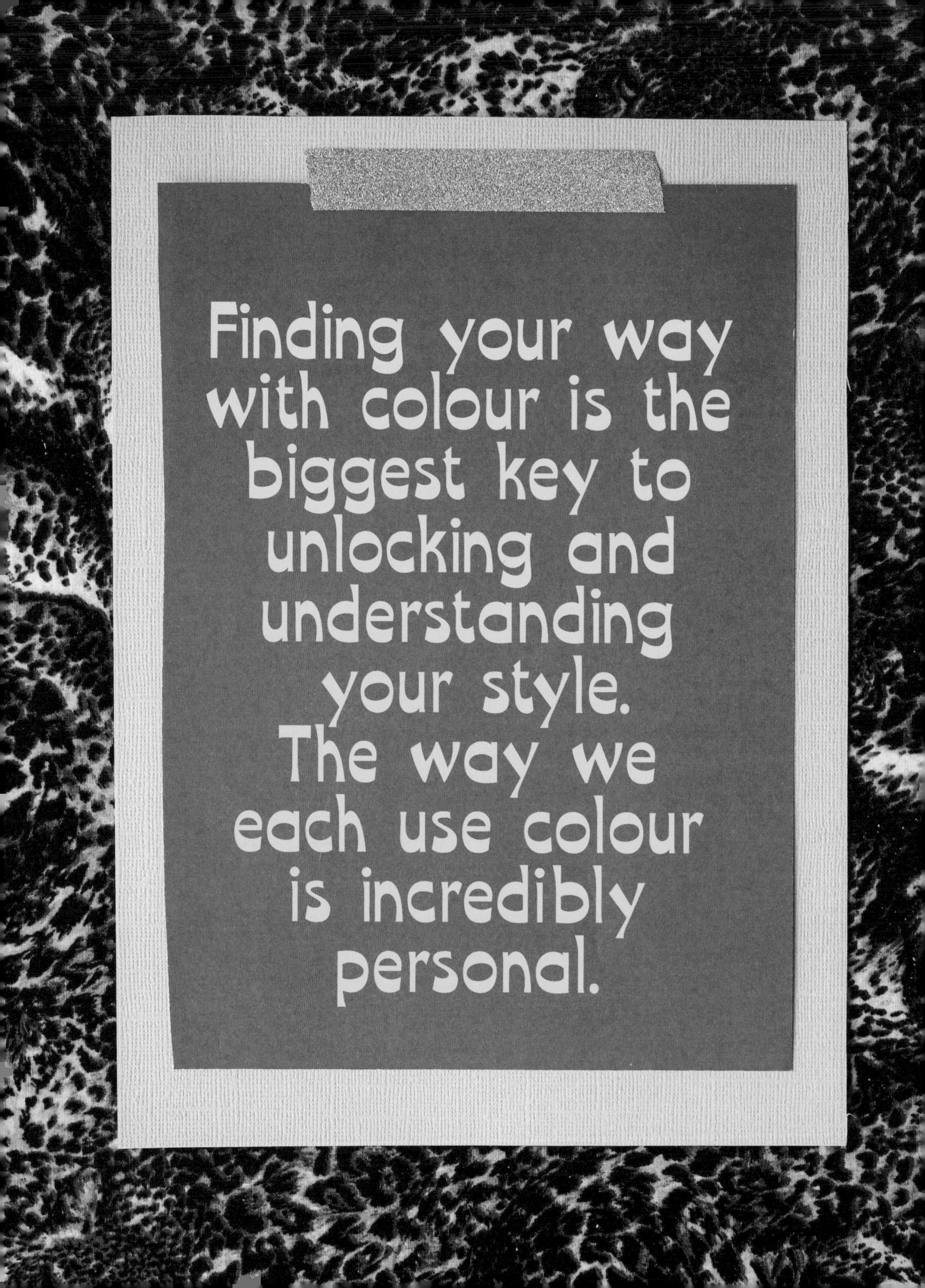

Finding your way
with colour is the
biggest key to
unlocking and
understanding
your style.
The way we
each use colour
is incredibly
personal.

That's a lot of different elements and it sounds chaotic (see why I can't put a label on it?) – so let's break that down to how I have approached it in my living space …

MORE WAYS TO EXPLORE YOUR STYLE

1 Mood Boards (overleaf)
Get back to basics with a good old mood board! Gather and save images that appeal to you – either online, physically or both. Go one step further than just picking the pictures and take some time to analyse what it is that appeals to you in each image and *why* – jot down these notes.

Mood boards can be textural and multidimensional. Collect fabric and paint swatches, even objects, to physically visualise the things you like. Seeing these as a collection really helps to make your style a tangible thing.

I'm a huge fan of Pinterest for storing and saving images to look back at again, but sometimes it can be overwhelming just how much is on there and it can be good to flick through a physical book or magazine instead.

2 Share It
Redesigning entire rooms isn't always possible, but if you're wanting to share your interior ideas or just use it as a creative outlet, try creating visuals like an online collage to share. These are a great way to try out ideas and colour schemes, as well as gain confidence in your abilities and distinct design voice.

Even just playing around sketching or collaging images of rooms can be a fun way to flex that design muscle.

3 Find Your People
Maximalists come in all forms, so find those that speak to your particular aesthetic. Here are just a few of my favourite designers to follow online (seriously, there are so many). Find out who your favourite accounts are following to discover new people to follow. Hashtags are another good way to find new faces too.

I give Instagram (and Pinterest) a lot of credit for developing my style, but that's just me. Living in a small country at the edge of the world, it is harder to find a range of people doing different things (not to say there isn't buckets of talent here in little ole NZ – there is, but the pool is much smaller). Sharing my home and finding others on social media has introduced me to and connected me with so many talented and creative people – not just in interiors but in every aspect of life.

It has also brought me opportunities (if that's something you're looking for!) and the days of an elite few being considered the only interior designers in town are well and truly over. You can do a lot within your own home and if you choose to share it with like-minded people, you may well find yourself with a new job. Whether you want to pursue it or not is up to you!

When it comes to inspiration, be sure to keep an open mind – I follow and enjoy plenty of accounts that aren't similar to me at all, but that's what I love and what keeps me inspired. It's also a reminder that creativity and self-expression come in many forms – from the food you cook, to the clothes you wear.

Stay true to yourself and use it to express what makes you unique, rather than a comparison sinkhole. If you find you're struggling to distinguish

Some of
my favourite

people online

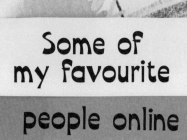

Gillian Bryce Gallery
@GillianBryce

Judy Aldridge
@atlantishome

Kate Pearce
@katepearcevintage

Natalie Papier
@Home_ec_op

It can be both satisfying and clarifying to gather together bits and pieces and see a scheme come together. Always try out the combinations you don't think will work to really push your ideas.

Follow your feelings and remember that you are not a trend page in a catalogue or magazine – you're a thinking, feeling person and the most important aspect to your own style is the stories you tell through the design of your home.

what ideas are your own – take a step back. Indulge or follow some new creative breadcrumbs to open your mind back up.

LOOK BEYOND INTERIORS

When you're looking at other interiors it can sometimes get confusing, differentiating what is truly your own style or just admiration (and trust me, I've had this conversation with some serious tastemakers who, despite having incredible personal style, still fall victim to a bit of 'the grass is always greener' design distraction).

There is a difference to admiring and being inspired, and realising that what you're feeling when you're looking at images is important. There are many beautiful rooms in this world and you won't like them all (or most for that matter),

but admiration is a lovely feeling and it can help considerably with your ability to maintain an open mind. Like going to an art gallery and still taking the time to look at artworks that don't instantly appeal to you; you learn, grow and better understand your own design sensibilities. Don't block off entire styles or designers just because you wouldn't design your own home as they do.

As with recognising what tells your story, become more aware of the art you love, TV shows, fashion, books, your favourite restaurant even – and consider how they potentially inform your style. Once you open your eyes to discovering your tastes and style in all these things, and acknowledge that you actually *do* already have your own unique design voice, you'll really find confidence and be able to stretch it and have fun with it.

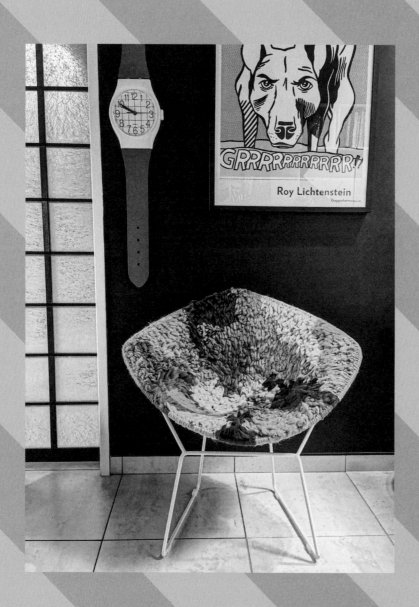

CHAPTER FOUR

Funda-
mentals

This room off our bedroom used to house a Jacuzzi – thankfully that was gone before we arrived, but we connected the two spaces with lush mauve carpet. Still a bit retro, just not as retro as a spa pool in the bedroom!

I AM GOING TO PRESS PAUSE FOR A CHAPTER AND GET PRACTICAL.

In creating our idyllic, personality-filled homes we often feel stifled by one massive thing – the house itself. If you are living in your absolute dream house, good for you, you can probably skip this chapter. But for most of us, we have restrictions. You might be renting, or living in a small apartment; you might have pre-existing design decisions you have to live with, or an outdated kitchen you don't have the budget to update.

We can look at all those lovely inspiration images we have saved to our mood boards and think, 'Well I don't live in an 18th-century cottage overlooking a lavender farm in the south of France, so why should I bother?' or 'How could I possibly take inspiration from that and apply that to my own home?' We can file those images away for the day we win the lottery and make those dreams come true, or we can work with what we've got now and make the best of it.

Every home, no matter how humble, deserves to be made as lovely as you want to make it.

I have a bit of a bee in my bonnet (and I don't even live next to a lavender farm yet) about the elitism that exists within design. So many eminent designers and owners of homes featured in design publications and TV shows come from generational wealth, and with that wealth they are afforded 'good taste'. We don't see nearly enough homes furnished with love, passion and ingenuity featured within the pages of magazines.

I don't want to use the phrase 'normal homes' because of course they are not normal – they are incredibly special. Is it not more impressive and delightful to walk into an unassuming brick bungalow and find an absolute haven of art and design, than to marvel at how tasteful a $20,000 sofa looks in a Georgian drawing room? Don't get me wrong,

More is more

I still love seeing those homes, but for those of us not to the manor born, it can feel like a level of style, or taste, we can't ever hope to attain. Which is of course, a load of nonsense that we need to get right out of our heads. Money can't buy style, or taste.

Now that we have established that most of us aren't living in the Venetian palaces we probably deserve, let's talk about the things in our home that are potentially outside of our control, or for now, outside of our ability to change.

Flooring

Flooring is something that can be very 'of its time', and not always in a good way. It is also costly to change. Most of us have a preference for the type of flooring we prefer and that is usually based on a mix of style, lifestyle (pets, kids, roller skates) and what we are used to.

I had never lived in a house with wall-to-wall carpet until we moved into the home my husband Sam and I live in now. In my mind it was the interiors equivalent of having cake for dinner – not classy but I wanted it so much. In general, aesthetically I don't love carpet – I love rugs atop of wooden floors; but sensory-wise it makes me melt in a way only a child who never had padded floors could. A soft carpet reminds me of rolling around at my grandparents' house, or sliding down the stairs at breakneck speed; it reminds me of playing Barbies at my friend Amy's house – in the bathroom, because they had carpet *everywhere* and it felt so luxurious.

I think my aversion to it comes from too many seas of grey carpets, endless runs of 'practical colours' that are the visual equivalent of white noise. There is often a real rejection around putting a rug on top of carpet: the carpet is soft so why would it need a rug?

I'll tell you why – because it looks nice. It grounds the room, adds interest and warmth, and breaks up colours. See page 128.

Have a dark carpet that's sucking light out of the room? Put a lighter or more colourful rug on top. Have a light carpet that is showing up every single little mark? Put a patterned rug on top.

When it came time to replace the worn carpet in our bedroom, I chose to stick with carpet. I didn't want to hop across cold floors on winter mornings. I chose a plush, pale lilac/pink carpet. Resale value be damned, *and* I have rugs on top of it. It's the best of both worlds.

Throughout most of our house we have large white ceramic tiled floors. They're not especially cool to look at but they sure are arctic to stand on, and slippery for pets and humans alike. The cost of redoing the flooring throughout the entire house isn't something we have the budget for at the moment, but I decided to cover the open-plan dining area with a pattern of coloured carpet tiles, that I cut and installed myself. They were easy to install, are super practical and have completely changed the space. They will also be easily removed without damaging the floor underneath and be able to be used elsewhere if I wanted.

All this is to say – there are ways around your flooring woes. Permanent or temporary, no matter your budget.

Kitchens and Bathrooms

Arguably the most important (and definitely most functional) rooms in the house, kitchens and bathrooms can be our biggest bugbear. You will see so many houses for sale or rent with a new kitchen installed, but new rarely means 'good'.

Have a dark carpet that's sucking light out of the room? Put a lighter or more colourful rug on top. Have a light carpet that is showing up every single little mark? Put a patterned rug on top.

They are often cheap, low quality and dull as dishwater but they're also brand-spanking new (or near enough) and difficult to justify ripping them out and starting again. Ditto bathrooms. I envy houses with genuinely old, worn-out kitchens and bathrooms that can be ripped out guilt free to start again with a blank slate.

If you're looking at your perfectly fine kitchen and seeking ideas for how to bring in personality, here are a few …

1 Paint your cabinetry – I painted my entire kitchen (walls, tiles and cabinets). Then I did the bathroom vanity and more recently I've painted the sink in the loo (yep, even the inside) using a specialised Dulux paint that has given it an enamel-like finish (they were laminate doors before). If you have solid timber doors (lucky you!) you can sand them back and refinish or paint using water-based enamel paint, the same you'd use on trims.

2 Alternatively, you can have cabinet doors wrapped with vinyl; the same goes for your fridge or dishwasher. Some places specialise in this technique for homes, but car vinyl places can often do it for you, or if you're feeling confident, you can do it yourself! Or use re-stickable wallpaper for a slightly more forgiving material to work with.

3 Replace the benchtop – often a new benchtop can freshen up the whole space. Combined with a lick of paint it can feel like an entirely new kitchen. Natural materials like stone, timber or bamboo make beautiful benchtops, but make sure you understand any upkeep required and think practically. Some marble and stone can stain, and timber can require re-oiling – just be sure that you're okay with that.

4 There are some amazing man-made materials now that are as hard-wearing and practical as they are beautiful. If you love colour, look into what places like Critical Design (in New Zealand) and Reddie (Australia) are doing with recycled plastics and glass for some fun options. Maybe you keep your cabinets white but splash out on a colourful recycled glass terrazzo benchtop?

5 Change out your splashback – splashbacks aren't generally huge areas so can be tiled affordably. Choose a tile that complements your existing benchtop using colour, texture or pattern and you'll find that it can make your benchtops look new too. Look for inspiration in kitchens with similar benchtops to what you're working with and see how other designers have teamed tiles with it. For the tiles in our kitchen, I couldn't find what I wanted at tile shops, so we installed black and white tiles that I then added coloured sections to for an entirely bespoke look.

6 Change up your handles – never underestimate the power of changing out handles, as sometimes that's all you need to give cabinets a new look. When I painted our bathroom vanity blue (overleaf), I opted for huge custom-made resin handles by New Zealand-based company Arc. The vanity itself was nothing special before, one of millions made I'm sure, but now it is one of a kind – can you see its robot face? I love that it has a face now!

Never underestimate the power of changing out handles, sometimes that's all you need to give cabinets a new look.

7 Wallpaper can be surprisingly hard-wearing in both kitchens and bathrooms, and you can coat it with a clear varnish to make it even easier to clean. Or even install a clear glass splashback over the top if you wanted to have it around a stove or sink area.

8 Install open shelves – this is an easy way to bring personality into a kitchen and can be achieved even with just one shelf rather than multiple if space doesn't permit. Use it to display your favourite dishes, cookbooks and vases. If you have more space, you could even extend this to be a free-standing shelving unit or glass-fronted cabinet. It can be especially nice to use pieces of furniture like this to break up the overwhelming functionality of a fitted kitchen.

9 If you have space for a bench or island in the middle, think about how that could be different from the rest of the kitchen while still making practical sense. I love seeing a kitchen with a reclaimed shop counter or cabinet turned into a kitchen island.

Doors and Windows

This is perhaps more about the larger issue of light and layout. We have all seen the renovation shows where they absolutely revolutionise a room by knocking a wall down and putting in some massive windows. Dreamy.

Where doors and windows are, and how large/small/beautiful they are, can have a lot to do with when our house was built. We want loads of light, but we also don't want to freeze to death (priorities) so prior to double glazing, architects and builders had to balance this. More modern houses can have a

lot more glazing (budget allowing) but it isn't always a case of the grass being greener – many large windows can leave rooms unbearably hot for parts of the year or accelerate fading of art and furnishings.

Given that, my first piece of advice here is going to be 'Come to peace with what you've got'. If drastically changing your windows isn't something currently on the cards, put it to the back of your mind. It comes around (again) to styling the home you have now and playing up the advantages. If you have a small dark room, assign it appropriately – a teenage bedroom, or paint it a deep colour to enhance its cosiness. A dark spot in your hallway could be the perfect place for a special artwork you want to keep out of direct sunlight, and instead can be lit up beautifully using a spotlight or lamps.

Arrange your furniture to make the most of both light and views – if you have any. I would love a house with a view, so when I see one and not a single seat in the house is soaking it in, I'm always surprised, even though it is absolutely none of my business whatsoever. It's a bit like those things we leave shut in the back of the cupboard – if we're not putting it in our eyeline to admire, we tend to forget all about it. Put your favourite chair in the best spot in the house, sit and have your morning coffee there, read a book on a Sunday afternoon there, or make it a corner for playing a family board game. Even if most of the time the cat is the one enjoying it, just having it set up like that will mean that you use it more.

Use blinds and curtains to enhance your windows. An age-old trick to making your windows appear bigger is to hang full-length curtains from the top of the wall, even if your windows only start 70 cm below that, and extend them down to the floor. Also, always be generous with curtains. A rule of thumb is

I do have a
tendency to fix
everything with
paint, but do
you know what?
It works.

Clockwise from top right: I'm always up for a disguise, here I used decorative fencing panels to make a cover for the outdoor heat pump unit; over summer I use our fireplace as a bit of a plant stand and use lamps to emulate that warmth, avoiding it feeling like a dead spot; inside I use a primer so that I can paint the heat pump units to match the walls and try and make them stand out a little less.

that your curtains should be one and a half times the width of your window, or at least two times for a fuller drape. Full curtains look opulent and luxurious.

If you have windows that look directly on to your neighbours, a full set of lightweight sheer curtains can look dreamy – letting in light while providing privacy.

While curtains require a lot of fabric, a beautiful roman blind can be a place to use a really special fabric or textile as you will need a lot less. More can most definitely be more, and you can absolutely have both a blind and curtains or use a double track to hang two sets of curtains. This can also be a great trick for winter where double curtains can do a fantastic job of keeping the cold out – a more practical pair behind and a decorative pair in front.

I make my own curtains, mostly because I'd rather spend my money on rugs and furniture, and because I'm impatient and want them done immediately. If you're able (or willing to learn) how to sew a straight line, you can sew your own curtains, I promise! YouTube is a wealth of information on step-by-step instructional videos for projects like this.

The Other Ugly Practical Stuff

Here I'm talking mostly about the things that keep us warm or cool: air conditioning units, radiators, wall heaters, fireplaces and wood burners (they're not that ugly but I'm going to lump them in anyway).

I love our heat pumps – they make our house hugely more comfortable in both winter and summer, but damn, they are ugly and often quite big. The 'designer' ones are somehow even more ugly, only drawing attention to their presence by being glossy black or red with chrome accents. To be efficient they have to be in prominent positions and when

your walls are a beautiful colour, a stark white heat pump unit stands out like a sore thumb. However, they do a good job and I'd still much rather be with them than without.

I do have a tendency to fix everything with paint, but do you know what? It works. A few years ago, I painted the indoor heat pump unit with a plastic primer and then wall paint to match the walls. It worked like a dream and then I proceeded to paint on top of it at least three more times as I changed the wall colour. Just be sure to mask the vents and sensors carefully and check with your installer if it's still under warranty.

Outside I used metal garden panels to create a cover for the external unit that could be lifted off over winter to maintain efficiency, when we weren't out on the deck looking right at the ugly thing!

Fireplaces are the most wonderful things in winter, and honestly nothing beats the warmth from a real fire. Through summer and spring though, they stand awkwardly in the room, cold and unloved, just waiting for a chilly day. I personally struggle with an empty fireplace (okay, an empty anything!) and when not in use I adorn our wood burner with plants and lamps, to create a cosy focal point in the room – even if it's not needed to produce heat. Layering indoor plants of varying heights and textures and using pots and vases that connect to the rest of the room stop it becoming a 'dead zone' for half of the year. You can't hide it and you can't remove it, so why not make the most of it being there?

These might not be the problems you're necessarily trying to solve, but I hope they can serve as inspiration for how you can improve those things that niggle you!

CHAPTER FIVE

Colour + pattern

Colourful textiles and accessories
are the easiest way to inject colour
and pattern into your home without
making big changes.

I BELIEVE EVERYBODY ALREADY HAS THEIR COLOUR PALETTE AND DEEP DOWN THEY KNOW IT TOO.

Being bold with colour and pattern is all about ignoring trends, creating your own colour story, and embracing the magic of letting loose and playing with patterns that inspire you and make you feel good.

Colour

The Colours are Within You

I don't know if it's just me, but finding your colour palette has been made to feel like some kind of medical assessment. I keep seeing videos online of anxious-looking people being draped in swatches of fabric by an expert, only for the expert to look at the camera and tell us how truly awful this colour is for

them: that they look ill, or dead or zombified. It's eye-rolling, because the diagnosis being given is often that you actually suit a more pastel yellow, but at the same time it just feeds into this idea that most of us don't understand colour. And that is just absolute nonsense. I believe everybody already has their own colour palette, and with that an understanding of colour – it's just been buried underneath all that rubbish we have been told, and believed to be true.

Think about children and their unabashed love of colour. In fact, most young kids consider their current favourite colour to be the most important information they need to hand over after their own name. They share their favourite colours so boldly and passionately that tears and fights around crayon use, or the colour of a T-shirt are pretty common. When do we lose that confidence and conviction?

I don't believe we do. I think most adults just squash it down inside themselves. Why? Because we're bombarded with trends and that potentially poisonous word 'taste'. We are told what's good and what's bad; what's classy and what's restful; and what's garish and what's loud; and it crushes us down until all that comes out is a fear of colour and yet another grey sofa, and magazines filled with homes that are impossible to tell apart.

Finding your colour palette isn't necessarily about hiring a colour specialist to plant, water, grow and birth your colours into existence, but rather allowing yourself to sink into colours you already know and love. Then from there, discovering and experimenting with new ones; collecting combinations, testing how they make you feel, discarding the ones that don't resonate and having a play with those that do.

Here is a simple activity to help you get a grasp on your own colour story …
Take yourself shopping for colour. Head to a beautiful online store you love and start adding to your cart. You're not buying anything; nothing needs to fit or be practical – just go on instinct. Don't overthink it and don't hold back! If you're scrolling past something and it makes you go 'ooh', then add it – do not even think about 'Would I wear it?', we are tapping into gut instinct here. When you have 10-plus items saved, take a screenshot of your cart and analyse the colours you see.

Another way you can practise this is by grabbing a big set of pencils, crayons or paints and just blocking the colours you're drawn to onto a piece of paper.

You will soon see patterns in the colours you gravitate towards – the ones that make you feel good, as well as those that are more daunting to you.

A couple of tips to help stretch your colour boundaries beyond the basics …
You have figured out your key colours, the ones you feel comfortable with, and you know you love. Now it's time to push past that and widen your palette.

All of the websites listed below generate colour palettes around specific shades, or can generate them from an uploaded image that resonates with you. The options are limitless though, so save your favourites and have a think about why you love them. Add these to your mood board and consider how you could include these colours in your life.

Websites
* Coolors.co
* Colorhunt.co
* Mycolor.space

Here are a few of my top modern books on colour if you feel like nerding out and learning more …
* *The Anatomy of Colour* by Patrick Baty
* *The Secret Lives of Colour* by Kassia St. Clair
* *Colour: A Visual History* by Alexandra Loske

Start Your Own Library
Pinterest or Instagram (or both) are amazing ways to save colour combo inspiration (which, remember, can come from anywhere – a packet of chips, a red car next to a pink skip – start looking and you won't be able to stop). Don't just gather images though – have a play at trying some of these colour combinations out. It doesn't have to be on a large

My favourite
books on colour

Playing with colour combinations is my happy place.

scale – a small collection of objects, pieces of fabric, coloured paper, etcetera can all be used to try colours together. Look for how a colour changes depending on what it is paired with, and what combinations really 'sing' for you.

You can (and should!) play with colour everywhere and anywhere – even as you prepare dinner (hello beetroot and feta dip on everything). It will only make life more fun while strengthening your eye. I often take photos on my phone of colour combinations that catch my eye and I want to remember. They're often not great photos, or even necessarily beautiful things, but I recognise something in the way the colours work together that makes me want to document it.

Pick up paint chips every time you're in the hardware shop. Having your own little colour library is the easiest way to get a feel for colours you don't (yet) have in your own home. Colour is all about doing and seeing, so stop dreaming and start playing.

Most importantly, be like that four-year-old with the crayons. Be bold, be brave, be really opinionated.

Don't shy away from having opinions on colour. For example, you say you'll never wear yellow, but why? There is no such thing as just yellow, there are thousands of yellows! What types of yellow do you like the least? Do you like orangey yellows like marigold? How about greeny yellows like chartreuse? How does the yellow make you feel?

All these questions will help you better understand colour and your relationship with it, and the more you know the more confident you feel. But with that, be open to change. As a teen I vowed I would never wear pink – what a fool I was because now pink is one of the very best colours in my world. We all go through colour phases, I suppose you might even call them trends, and I have fun indulging them by trying them out by painting a room or bringing in art or accessories in that colour. I know, however, that I have certain colours I'll almost always include and know I'll love – you can probably guess them just from the images in this book, but generally they are oranges and pinks. I come back to them again and again in different ways.

Now you are feeling a bit more confident with your ability to know what colours you like and your confidence to pick them, let's talk more practically about choosing and using colour in your home – particularly when painting walls.

Swatch Sideways

When comparing swatches, we often pick our colour and then compare a lighter and a darker shade of that colour. That's also how lots of paint sample cards and swatch books are set up – with colours of a similar tone ordered from light to dark. It makes sense from an organisational point, but not necessarily from a colour-picking one.

As a teen I vowed I would never wear pink — what a fool I was because pink is one of the very best colours in my world.

Instead of looking up and down, look to the side!
Firstly, compare swatches of similar colours from slightly different parts of the spectrum – some warmer and some cooler. Then you will be sure that the hue is right. Once you have this nailed, you can figure out the shade, or darkness. You need to get the colour you want!

For example, if I'm choosing a peachy-pink to act almost as a warm neutral without appearing too pink, I'd consider colours with a pink base, a more orange base, and even a brown base and compare those as swatches on the wall before narrowing down how dark or light it needs to be.

Colour Changes

Colours can look drastically different on the wall, depending on the type of light the room receives (both natural and artificial), how much light, and whether that light is warm or cold. Also consider when the room gets the most sunlight – is it catching lots of bright morning sun, or warmed through with the sunset? Is it a room you mostly use at night, or throughout the day? It sounds like a lot to consider, but it really is as simple as painting or sticking some samples on the wall, preferably in a couple of different spots so you can see how the colours look in both a dark corner and near a window.

Some paint companies offer larger-sized paint samples that you can order online and stick to the wall. Or make your own using sample pots and some sheets of cardboard. Once you have narrowed down your options with these, you can move onto test pots of your final two or three colours. Paint the largest samples you can. If you're just doing a stroke, you may as well save the hassle and stick up a swatch.

Not all Colours are Created Equal

Pigment is a wonderful thing, but varying pigments behave differently. This isn't so much a warning,

just a heads-up so you don't get disheartened if you need to paint more coats than you were anticipating. Rich jewel tones like dark blues and reds will almost always need a coat or two more than their softer counterparts. Generally, the more white a colour contains, the more opaque (solid) it will apply. This is also a general rule when it comes to the quality of paints, as often (but not always), more expensive paint brands have a higher percentage of pigment in their paints, so they should take more coats. Worth thinking about if you're the one doing the painting!

There's Nothing to be Afraid of

For all intents and purposes, paint is almost always temporary. Anything you don't like can be changed or painted over with a tin of paint and a few hours, so what's the harm in trying something new? If you have followed the steps above to choose the perfect colour, hold your nerve (and your paint roller) and get that colour on the walls. Anything that's a big change will have you feeling a bit wobbly somewhere in the process – we're creatures of habit after all (honestly, I still get a shock from my reflection every time I get my eyebrows done). Remember that painting a wall is only the first layer of your room; adding your furniture, art, accessories, curtains and lighting will all work to bring it together. So, don't freak out!

Be Passionate About Paint

There is nothing else that is as cost-effective and yet makes such a big impact as paint. Think of walls as the canvas to create your room on top of and do the best job you can – and trust me, you can do a great job! Tools matter with painting, so get the best paint, masking tape, brushes and rollers you can afford.

Prep
(So boring, but so worth it)

CLEAR THE ROOM
Remove as much furniture as possible. For heavy items, move them to the centre of the room and cover with drop cloths. You want to have space to move around and fewer things to get messy.

✳

CLEAN THE WALLS
Wipe down walls with a damp cloth to remove dust and grime. Let them dry completely. A wall might look clean but dust and grease will affect how your paint goes on.

✳

REPAIR IMPERFECTIONS
Use spackle (putty filler) and a putty knife to fill holes or cracks. Once dry, sand smooth with fine-grit sandpaper.

✳

TAPE EDGES
Apply painter's tape along baseboards, trim, and the ceiling edge to ensure sharp lines. I use a credit card to run over the edge of my tape to really seal it.

✳

PRIME
If changing from a dark to a light colour, or painting on a shiny surface, applying primer is going to be helpful.
If you're just painting regular interior walls that have already been painted, you won't need to prime.

Painting
(the fun bit)

MIX THE PAINT
Stir the paint well to ensure colour consistency. If the lid is secured well, give it a really good shake for a couple of minutes.

✳

CUT IN
Using a brush, paint around the edges of the room, around taped areas, windows and doors. If you have a steady hand you might prefer to cut in without using tape – especially in older houses where nothing is straight, this can sometimes look neater. Try it out and see what you prefer.

✳

USE THE ROLLER
Pour paint into the tray and roll the roller back and forth in the tray's well to coat it evenly without having it dripping with paint. Start from the ceiling down to avoid drips. Apply paint in a 'W' pattern for even distribution, then fill in without lifting the roller to avoid paint lines or obvious strokes.

✳

SECOND COAT
Allow the first coat to dry completely before applying a second coat (or third if necessary).

✳

REMOVE TAPE
Gently remove your tape at a 45-degree angle to the wall before the paint fully dries to avoid peeling any paint off.

Don't expect to be a colour master right away. Mistakes are good!

A Few More Tips

✶ Avoid Drips – Avoid overloading your brush or roller with paint to minimise drips.

✶ Keep a Wet Edge – Always paint from wet to dry areas to blend the edges and avoid streaks.

✶ Take Your Time – Don't rush, especially with prep work. A well-prepped room makes painting easier and the results more professional.

Walls are Just the Beginning

Don't overlook your trim. Defaulting to white door and window frames can really break up a scheme. Continuing a wall colour on to the frames (but remember to use a primer, an enamel paint for trims) looks really smart and also makes a room look bigger. Think of your ceiling as a fifth wall, and choose a colour that accentuates the room rather than detracts from it. The best use of paint is using it with conviction. Colour drenching (where the entire room is drenched in a colour, ceilings and all) is something we continue to see more of, and it makes for such an enveloping space. Alternatively, how about a contrasting ceiling with a statement light fitting? Painting your rooms in this way doesn't have to mean dark and moody, or super bright. It can be just as effective with lighter, more muted tones too.

Working with colour is all about confidence and as with anything, the more we do that thing, the more we show, the more confidence we get. Don't expect to be a colour master right away. Mistakes are good! How do we know what we love if we don't try things out? It's a lot like cooking – as your confidence grows, you try new combinations, make a couple of inedible meals – learn what you do and don't like and really stretch your own reading of colour until you are fluent and fearless and throw away the recipe book!

If you're still feeling a little stuck, start with a room you don't 'live' in – a laundry, bathroom or hallway – and allow yourself complete carte blanche. Live with it a while and see how it makes you feel. There are some truly bonkers little powder rooms out there – and why not? Almost everyone visits it, but few stay too long (I mean, hopefully) so why not make a statement?

Pattern

For most of my childhood, we were lucky to live next door to Diane – a professional cake maker, and owner of a convertible white jeep – and her lovely husband Edward and fluffy dog Poppy. Diane's own children were grown up and I'd go over to her house for solo sleepovers to get away from all my younger siblings and get treated like a queen.

Diane's house was (and I'm sure still is) a beautiful old cottage, all wobbly beams and low ceilings, plush furniture and … did you guess? … absolutely bursting with Laura Ashley-esque florals. The guest room I'd stay in had floral wallpaper up the walls and over the ceiling, and if my memory is correct, it even had matching curtains – it was SO over the top and just completely luxurious. I loved it. Getting tucked in there at night felt like going to sleep in a doll's house.

For as long as I can remember I have looked for pattern-repeats in fabrics and wallpapers, or for hidden motifs and shapes, as a way to distract and calm myself when I'm upset. I do it with everything that might have a pattern: tiles, bricks, laminate flooring – if there's a repeat I'll spot it. It's a little puzzle I can do. If you spot me staring at a wall, that's probably what I'm doing!

Designing surface patterns is one of my most favourite parts of the work I do nowadays. Somehow turning an anxious habit into a marketable skill feels very successful, even if I'm just as anxious as ever.

Jokes and mental health issues aside, it's no surprise that I connect pattern so strongly with a sense of home and find comfort in being surrounded by them.

Just like art, there are certain patterns and motifs that resonate with us on a more personal level – the ones that evoke a feeling or a memory. Then there are those that visually please or excite us – they're not necessarily nostalgic but they make us feel good. That might be because you find them pretty, or that they have a structure and order that calms your mind, or maybe just that you love the colours.

Lastly, there are patterns that say nothing to us; we consider them safe and inoffensive – I want you to try and eliminate this last section from your home (and while you're at it, why not your wardrobe too).

Pattern Mixing, Matching and Clashing

Mixing, matching and clashing patterns is arguably one of the most difficult and coveted elements of design. It feels a bit like juggling – get it right and you will be asked to perform it at parties. Get it wrong and there's nowhere for your eyes to rest.

Like with colour, practice is key, and even more important when it comes to perfecting working with pattern, is being willing and unashamed to make mistakes. The truly brilliant pattern combinations are those that are one small step from being a hot mess – they look like they shouldn't work … yet they do. How? It's not entirely magic, though it can feel like it sometimes, but there are links between the patterns that may seem invisible at first glance, but they are still there and that is the trick.

How far you want to go depends on your love of pattern and how bold you want to be. Of course, I assume you're a super bold pattern-clashing queen.

Here are a few guidelines that can help you get started mixing patterns like a pro.

Start with the Basics

Start with a block colour, and then add a simple stripe or check – this is foolproof, it will always work so long as your stripe or check is either black and white or the same colour as your plain (we can branch

The easiest patterns to start with are stripes and checks, they go with anything! Add a stripe next to a

solid colour, and then try finding a floral or abstract design that includes one of those colours to tie them together.

Just like art, there are certain patterns and motifs that resonate with us on a more personal level – the ones that evoke a feeling or a memory.

out with colour more once we're comfortable). Then add to that a more adventurous pattern. This could be a floral or an abstract, depending on your taste. At first, ensure there is a colour link between the three elements. This basic combo of three is an instant pattern mix and easy to achieve and hard to mess up. From there you can then add more elements and flex the boundaries.

Colour

Unify with colour, play around with a strong colour link and then with much more obscure ones. Sometimes, it's just a touch of a colour that unites a family of patterns. Think of patterns you put together as being cousins rather than siblings (unless of course you're going for some floor-to-ceiling chintz realness, yass queen!). For example, you might have Pattern A share a colour or style link with Pattern B but share nothing directly with Pattern C. Pattern B shares one attribute with A and one with C and so links them together without them being cut from the same cloth (literally!). Using patterns like this gives a looser, more relaxed scheme. It's more fun, looks more organic and gives you more scope design-wise. The tighter we confine our colour and pattern palettes the more trapped we feel and the harder it is to flourish in your design.

In short, keep your options open! It's also a great way to incorporate pieces you really love that might not seem to fit.

Scale

Be like the three bears. Scale is probably the most important factor to consider when mixing patterns. In general, combining different scales of patterns will be the most successful, and avoiding all patterns of a similar scale – which can visually compete for attention rather than working together. For starters try and decorate like the three bears – one big, one medium, and one small-scale pattern.

The Pièce de Résistance

The ultimate trick to an impressive pattern mix is to add the final piece of the puzzle – the wild card! Having a piece in there that seems completely disconnected to the others will add that magic ingredient. Figuring out what this random piece should be is something that comes with trial and error. That is, practice you can do right then and there. Switch things out, try a pattern from a piece of clothing or fabric swatches, or whatever you have to hand. And go by feel. You will know something is right when everything around it suddenly looks more intentional, more fun, more comfortable. See page 120 for my case study on pattern mixing.

Floral
+
Floral
(scales/eras)

Pattern combinations to try

You can practise these by adding combinations to an online shopping cart or Pinterest board.

Botanical
+
Stripes

Pictorial
+
Abstract

Traditional
+
Modern

Ethnic or
Antique Textiles
+
Modern

Animals
+
Geometric

Case Study – Pattern Mixing

1 Let's quickly look at how these patterns hang together using the principles discussed. Firstly, if you have wallpaper, then inevitably that will always be your starting point as it was for me here.

3 From there, the cushions echo various aspects of the above. The stripe reflects and balances the strong black line of the throw, which is important to help keep the eye moving when you have a real show stealer like that.

A similar black line can be seen in the striped and face cushions. The black stripe echoes the stripes within the clock fabric, while the face cushion shares that use of a strong, dark line in a different way. The red cushion acts as the wild card piece and ensures the whole combination looks cooler and less contrived. When in fact, it's picking up the red from other cushions.

2 From the wallpaper, I chose to pick up the yellow, as well as the leaf motif in the yellow banana leaf bedding. That is a pretty solid and obvious pattern match that works on its own, but falls pretty flat as far as interest and layering goes.

So, then I needed to add in my twist – which is where the clock pattern comes in. It takes the yellow from the bedding, but also the mauve that is in the background of the wallpaper, but then heads in a totally new direction – with the graphic line, the contrast of the subject matter, and additional colours of peach and rusty brown.

Everything is linked but not so it's immediately obvious. Each piece brings an extra layer to the story of the room.

CHAPTER SIX

Layout + lighting

I'm an absolute sucker for a great
lampshade and how a simple change
can make a big impact on a room.

LAYOUT AND LIGHTING ARE EVERYTHING.

You can have the most beautiful home in the world but if you have rubbish lighting, and a layout which doesn't enhance the space or how you live, then it will never look as wonderful as you want it to.

Layout

ARRANGING A ROOM

'A room' is obviously a very broad term. The layout of a living room is vastly different to a bedroom, but some main principles apply. These points should give you a good idea of how to best arrange any room to be both fit for purpose and appealing to the eye.

1 Fresh Eyes
Often we default to putting furniture in the most obvious place, or where the previous owners had it – I've done this plenty! – so approach each room with fresh eyes. Why not have the couch in the middle of the room if that is where it will offer the best view/allow you to snuggle up in the sun ... just because it hasn't been done before doesn't mean it can't be done.

2 Will You Use it?
Think really hard about how you *actually* live. This is important and you have to be honest with yourself. Do you regularly entertain 12 people? Or is the dining table more of a dumping ground and you like to eat in front of the television, in which case does it need to be front and centre?

3 Prioritise
Design spaces that fit *your* way of living. That might mean doing away with a dedicated dining room and creating a TV snug or home office; or switching rooms around to make space for your banquet table. It's your space – you can (and should) use it as you want!

4 Consider the Immoveable First

Fireplaces, windows and doors basically. Where's the daylight coming from? What do you want to look at? Don't consider the TV an immovable feature – it can be a real faff to move, yes, but sometimes that's what a room needs most! Think about how you move through the space. If it is leading to another room, do you want a clear open flow, or a more contained separate set-up?

5 Size and Proportion

Huge couches that are out of proportion with the size of the room look awful. If they loom over everything else, that's a turd you just can't polish no matter how many throws you try to disguise it with. Again, you have to be brutally honest with yourself. If something looks too big or too small, then it just is. Try it in another room if it's something you really love.

6 It Doesn't Have to go Against the Wall

This is a biggie. Often it is a necessity to have your sofas butted up to the walls, but it all comes down to proportion. If you're all sitting a thousand miles from each other around the outside of the room like wallflowers at the prom ... something is wrong. Look at the Queen – she had her sofas arranged in the middle of the room in intimate settings, with pieces like sideboards and cabinets against the walls. I don't know if you live in a stately home, I'll presume not, but the rule applies to us plebs too. If you have a bit of space behind your sofa, it's a great spot for a narrow table to hold lamps, flowers and cups of coffee.

7 Rugs – Go Big

Get the biggest rug for a space you can fit and afford. Or consider layering with rugs. Small rugs floating in the middle of the floor just generally look too small (proportion again). Ideally all your main furniture should be able to sit on the rug, or at least (and more realistically) the front legs. If your rug is too small, put it at the end of your bed, or in a smaller room. Rugs aren't just for hard floors either. No matter how new your carpet is, it will probably still look nicer with a rug on top. Rugs define spaces and areas, they add colour and pattern to a large blank surface – they are not purely about warmth. Flat weave rugs like kilims are perfect on top of carpets because the carpet grips them in place.

8 Artwork

When it comes to art, it once again comes back to proportion and really thinking about scale and how an artwork interacts with the space. Consider using a piece of art as the focal point of your room and prioritise that. Don't hang your pictures too high on the wall, and if in doubt go lower. In lots of rooms, we are mostly sitting down when we see art, and even when standing, the average sightline isn't as high as you think.

9 Lighting

Maximalists don't use the big (main) light, unless it's a civil defence emergency, and I have got a lot to say about lighting so let's go into lighting in a bit more detail in the next section.

10 Wardrobe

Have an unusual space? Put something unusual inside it. This round brick room (top left and page 103) was designed as an office by the original owner. I had thought it could be a movie room, but the reality was, we didn't need one. What I *did* need was space for my other passion – fashion. Sharing a wardrobe with Sam was a mess, so why not use this odd space for something wonderful! It was an affordable change – I had a metal worker make and install two curved rails and I took the door off the cupboard to create a shoe closet. It's completely bonkers but it just makes sense – for me!

Have an
unusual space?
Put something
unusual
inside it.

Choose one room in your home that has always been arranged in the same way (I recommend a living room or dining room) and try something new. Focus on the main layout of the room, don't worry (unless you're inspired!) about changing art, power points ... just yet.

✳

Then, I want you to live with the new layout for the next week. Feel free to make more changes but mostly just notice what you like/don't like about it. After the week you can go back to how you had it if you want, but I think you'll find you will adopt some of the changes or be inspired to try others. I'd love to know what you find!

A Challenge for You — Try a New Layout

Most rooms can be arranged in ways that can create a completely different feel, from ultra-modern to formal, or from a sophisticated conversation spot to the ultimate comfy TV-watching haven.

A space can be whatever you want it to be; one woman's lounge is another woman's boudoir.

Case Study Over the Years, Same House, Same Room

✳ A space can be whatever you want it to be – one woman's lounge is another woman's boudoir. My lounge has changed significantly over the years. The first iteration was based entirely on how the home was set up when we viewed it. As we lived in it and got to know it, we recognised how we were using the spaces, or more importantly, the spaces that weren't being used.

✳ There are different reasons this happens – one might be that you feel like you need a dedicated dining area, but you always eat in the lounge. Or that your bedroom gets all the afternoon sun while your living room is in darkness.

✳ For us, our 'dining room' was the only room in the house with doors opening directly onto the deck and back garden. Year-round it had lovely light and a wonderful view, which was really nice for the unused table and chairs that took up all of the space in there! As much as I'd like to say we have civilised conversations over the dinner table each night, the reality is Sam and I almost always eat on the sofa. For a change I turned the dining room into a snug (a small living room), perfect for cosy TV in the evening but equally as lovely in the daytime, with views to

Then

the garden. The dining table doesn't appear as formal in its new position near the kitchen, but not only is it much more practical – it actually gets more use.

✳ I was in a strong mid-century vibe when we first moved into this house and echoed similar houses I had seen in the décor. Though this felt too rigid for me. Our house was built in the 1980s and is an homage to many styles; it didn't need to be museum worthy. I was trying out a more pared-back way with design, but ultimately it didn't feel very me. Every version is a learning experience though, and there are aspects of this room I still echo (or have!). The Robin Day moulded dining chairs are something I still own and love – their utilitarian practicality, comfort and retro style still hit the right note for me. And while I now have a stone dining table, I realised that a round table is something that I really love for conversation with friends.

✳ Creating the snug. I made this change during the lockdowns of 2020 – we were stuck at home and comfort was key. I found myself really leaning into the design influences of more traditional and old-fashioned eras – Arts and Crafts, the Bloomsbury Group, English country interiors. At a time when the world felt very changed and unknown, I returned to my roots – to a room that looked and felt like 'home'.

Now

PATTERN ♡

✳

LOVE!

Blues

Finding the perfect shade for a
vintage lamp is so satisfying. This stripy
one in my laundry is made from fabric
by Sophie Robinson for Harlequin.

Lighting

In my experience, lighting is the most overlooked feature in homes, but it's also the easiest to inexpensively correct too. While a lighting designer and an expensive fit-out can work wonders, quite honestly so can a few lamps (and if you have seen my house, I have, um, more than a few).

The warm light cast by lamps doesn't just make your room look cosy and lovely, it is also proven to be good for your health and contribute to better sleep. Harsh overhead lighting is just that – harsh. So treat yourself to living in a softer glow. Here are my top 10 tips and tricks to get you started:

1 Lamps aren't just for bedrooms and lounges
I love a lamp in a hallway, the kitchen and the bathroom (safely of course). It might seem weird to put lamps somewhere like a kitchen which is a high-traffic, hardworking area but it is a wonderful way to change the mood and set the tone. After dinner is cooked and the kitchen cleaned (in theory), switching off the overhead lights and having lamps for any evening-treat-foraging or tea-making really marks the end of the working day and the time to chill out. Stop shining a spotlight on work to be done tomorrow and bask in the evening glow.

An LED strip light running under the lower edge of a bathroom vanity or kitchen cabinets is a great way to softly light areas for night-time.

2 Spread it Out
When choosing and positioning lamps, you still want to make sure light is distributed around the room. The primary focus is where people sit and need to be able to see what they're doing, but you also want to provide at least some light in all four corners of a room so that the room is lit. It doesn't need to all be super bright, working-level light – just enough that you no longer need to turn on the overhead lights.

3 Illuminate Features
As well as lighting a room, use lamps or lighting to draw focus to an artwork, a styled shelf or a console table. Think about how you could softly light bookshelves or a small nook. I love a light that casts upwards to illuminate art on the wall and often have a lamp or two sitting on the floor to achieve this. My favourite lighting sources for this are the Philips Hue Go lamps which are also portable – so you can use them in the centre of a table for a dinner party without the need for a cord. You will find a couple of these tucked around various corners of my home, lighting little vignettes.

4 Levels and Layers
Lighting needs to be on different levels, both height- and depth-wise to achieve a well-distributed and pleasing glow. Standard, or floor lamps are essential and a great way to make a feature of potentially dead space too. Try putting a table lamp in front of a floor lamp and doubling up. It is a really effective way to create some great lighting. Once you have put lamps in the obvious places, stand back and assess and try lamps in additional spots – borrow lamps from other rooms while you play around.

Learning the type of light that feels good for you is an art in itself, and often overlooked, but when you nail it and you walk in at the end of a hard day it will instantly make you feel better. It's worth continuously curating and refining your lighting scheme.

5 Task Lighting
Task lighting is essential in areas where you need to be able to see what you're doing (who'd have thought), like reading, cooking or working. Desk lamps, under-cabinet lights and floor lamps next to seating areas ensure these spots are well lit without overpowering the rest of the room's cosiness.

Never underestimate the power of natural light for making a home feel warm and welcoming.

Clockwise from left: Our home doesn't have a big garden, but it is surrounded by greenery; shadow play from plants is like a temporary wallpaper during the golden hour, my camera roll is full of it; there is a trend for strong direct light, but I'd choose dappled light anytime.

Choose lights with adjustable heads or arms to give you the flexibility to direct light exactly where you need it, enhancing functionality without sacrificing warmth. I'm a fan of a traditional Anglepoise lamp for just that reason!

6 Don't Forget Your Biggest Light

Never underestimate the power of natural light for making a home feel warm and welcoming. During the day, maximise natural light. Sheer curtains can diffuse sunlight, filling your room with a soft, natural glow that's both uplifting and cosy. In the evenings, the warm, ambient indoor lighting takes over, maintaining that snug feel. You're not trying to light your evening home to make it feel like it does during the day – that's impossible. Embrace, emphasise and capitalise on the different personalities daytime versus night-time brings to your home.

7 Using Mirrors for Light

Mirrors can amplify your lighting without adding more light sources. By placing mirrors opposite or near your light sources, you can reflect light around the room, making it feel brighter and more open while maintaining a cosy vibe. This trick works wonders in smaller spaces or rooms with limited natural light. A mirror placed opposite a window will bounce natural light around a room; think of them as secondary windows and place accordingly.

8 Light Bulbs

Probably the most important thing to consider is light bulbs! I am on a lifelong quest to find the perfect light bulbs. As we have moved more and more towards LED light bulbs – which are much better environmentally and economically – they struggle to match the warmth of an incandescent bulb, but they are getting better. Generally, having more lights at a low wattage (and always warm white) looks far better than a too-bright bulb. If you switch all your bulbs to LED, they're pulling much less power than traditional bulbs too.

I'm a big fan of smart bulbs where you can adjust the exact colour and brightness on your phone, but that can be expensive if you are doing a whole house, so it might be something to consider doing gradually, or just in a space you spend the most time in, like your lounge. The other brilliant thing about smart bulbs, switches or adapters (especially when you have a lot of lamps) is that you can set them to turn off via the app and create 'scenes' so you don't need to go round each night switching everything off! We have a 'good night' command that switches all the lamps off in the house apart from in our bedroom. Fancy.

9 Texture and Material Matter

The materials and finishes in your room can impact how light is absorbed or reflected. Materials like glass or polished metals reflect light while textured materials like wood and fabric can

Colours will also reflect back a colour which will impact your lighting (think of the yellow cast on your skin when you hold a buttercup up to your chin) and that will influence your lighting choices too.

soften the light, contributing to a cosier atmosphere. Similarly, darker colours absorb light while lighter ones reflect it. Colours will also reflect back a colour which will impact your lighting (think of the yellow cast on your skin when you hold a buttercup up to your chin) and that will influence your lighting choices too. For example, a blue room will probably look better with slightly warmer-toned light bulbs, than a pink room which would bounce a rosy glow.

10 Lamps and Lampshades

Shades are very important as they largely determine how the light will cast, and the colours they cast. Heavy shades offer much more up and down lighting, while more transparent shades will glow outwards.

Don't stick to the standard plain white shade either – lamps are one of best opportunities to add in a pattern. Finding great lampshades can be tricky, as most lamps come with a fairly plain shade, but you can easily have them made and as they use so little fabric you can go for something really special.

I get lots of lampshades from shops that make them, like Little & Fox in Napier in the North Island of New Zealand, and there are even places that have lampshade-making kits – have a look online. Love Frankie is a great source for shades in the UK, and Etsy has options all over the world.

Proportion between shade and base is so important, so make sure your shades aren't too small (the worst) or too big (the second worst), a shape that doesn't balance with the base, or doesn't cover up the fitting on the lamp (okay, maybe that is the worst). The best way to make sure of this is to carry your lamp along to wherever you're sourcing a shade from and try them out or get a professional opinion. Lampshade makers have a lot more ideas up their sleeve than just a plain drum shape (though sometimes that's just what you need!) and will consider finishing touches such as lining paper or fringing that can take your shade to the next level.

＊For those feeling crafty, there is a DIY project for how to cover an existing lampshade in Chapter Ten, Making (page 230).

Our home has these very warm-toned rimu ceilings, which are beautiful but really impact how colours appear as they cast a warm glow. Next left: embracing darker spots can make for cosy reading nooks (or cat corners). I like to use lamps to angle and direct light to make an impact.

THE
ART
MUSEUM

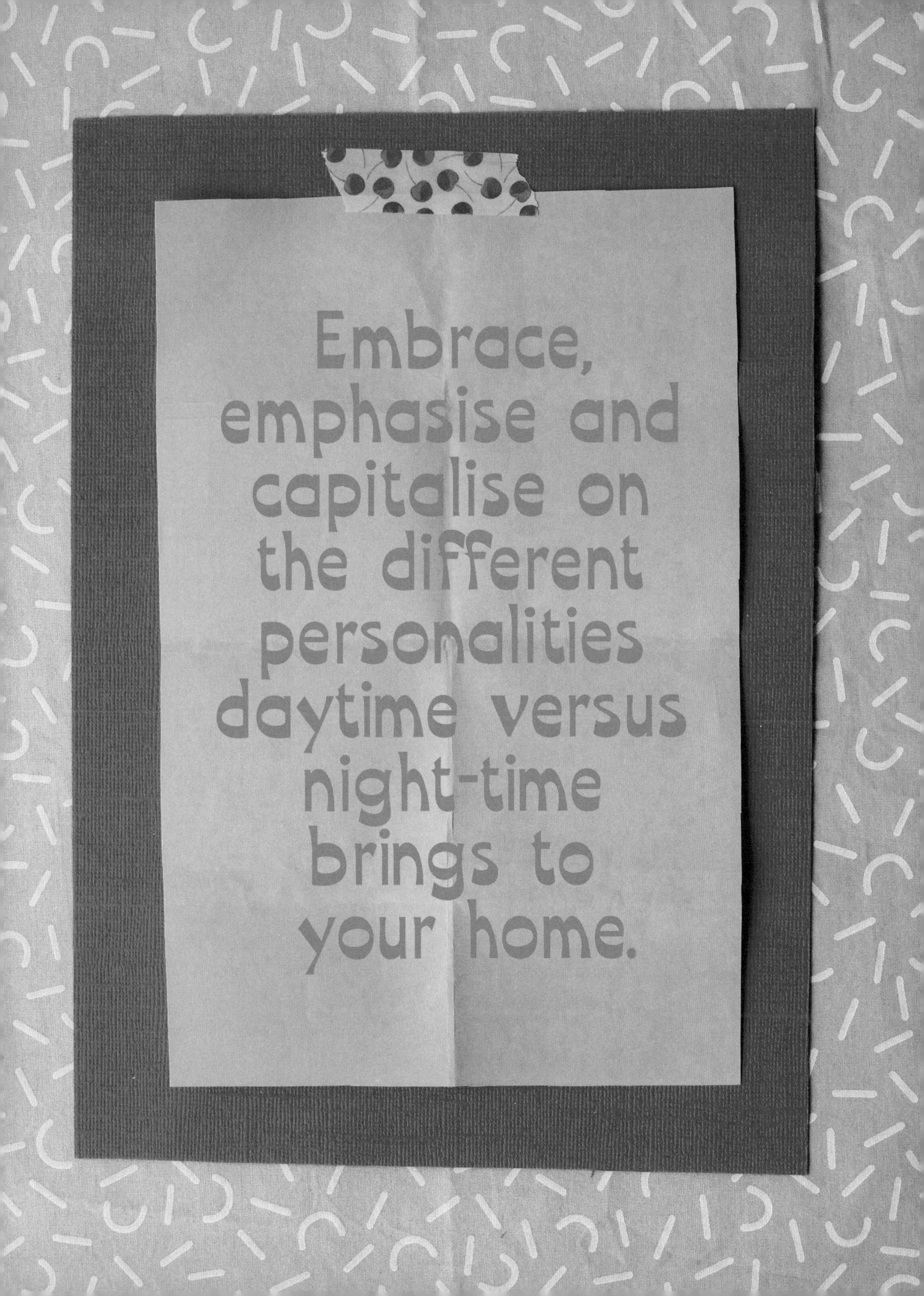

Embrace,
emphasise and
capitalise on
the different
personalities
daytime versus
night-time
brings to
your home.

CHAPTER SEVEN

Art

I'm a huge fan of a
coloured frame that
coordinates or contrasts
with the artwork inside.

ART IS ESSENTIAL TO ANY HOME, MAXIMALIST OR NOT ...

But a maximalist home without plenty of art is like a belt without a buckle – you can try and tie it together but it's going to fail. The good thing is art isn't just for the wealthy, and reframing what is and isn't art and how we use it in our homes opens up a whole world of wonderful design possibilities.

Growing up I was surrounded by art, and while none of it would be considered especially valuable in terms of money, it was invaluable in terms of shaping who I am.

Almost every school holiday I would go and spend a week or more with family friends, Sandra and Nick. Sandra was a professional photographer with her very own darkroom at home. She would lend me a camera and we'd go out together, taking photographs to process at home.

Like my mum, Sandra is incredibly creative and has always been interested in all sorts of different art – namely textiles and quilting which is where her main passions lie these days.

Sandra introduced me to lots of folk art, and I remember especially loving the naivety and simplicity of Shaker art and embroidery. Our holidays would be filled with creative projects and exploring in nature. We'd develop prints of my cat photographs and use them to inspire collages. Every day, we had a new art activity inspired by somewhere we went and the things we saw.

Sandra and Nick's house was full of beautiful art, black and white photographs beside antique embroidery samplers and painted landscape, woodcut prints and small sculptures dotted on shelves. On every bed in the house was a handmade quilt; art was everywhere.

I still see the influences of this home away from home, and it's a feeling I'm forever chasing. Of being somewhere where everything is special, and everything is loved. These holidays filled with creativity, fossil hunting, fishing forecasts, Enid Blyton at bedtime and cheese-and-pickle sandwiches

If you say it's art, it's art

eaten amongst abbey ruins … it is why I'll never be a one-large-artwork-and-done kinda girl – I want all these different feelings and mediums and snapshots to inspire me and make me feel at home.

One little project we did at the time together was to make a business card with a little black and white photo on it, name and occupation. I've been desperately trying to find mine, but it said *Artist, Photographer, Vet*, and while I didn't become a vet, I made a living from drawing and painting animals. How lucky am I? The impact of a home, and the art (both experienced and encouraged to create) stuck with me.

You may not be a nine-year-old girl reading this (or maybe you are! Hello!) but the art you put in your home matters to you, and it can also matter to those that are lucky enough to spend time with you. No generic big box store-printed canvases – let's make it count.

IF YOU SAY IT'S ART, IT'S ART
Don't get me wrong, I love a big magnificent painting, but budget doesn't always allow. However, I never let that be an excuse for empty walls – there are so many ways to create a statement away from traditional artwork.

Here are some of my favourite 'not art' art sources …
* Consider anything, and I mean *anything* you can fit in a frame – art. Posters, packaging, wallpaper or fabric samples, tea towels, silk scarves, second-hand books (covers or bookplates) all get elevated to art simply by popping them in a frame.

* Beautiful greeting cards and postcards (every single art gallery shop I visit I stock up) are easily and affordably framed as most are standard sizes. They also make great fillers for any smaller gaps in your

gallery wall if that's how you are displaying them. Or, collect a series and frame them to match for a larger statement.

* Beyond what fits inside a picture frame there's a whole myriad of other options that not only add interest but also texture. Small rugs, tapestries and wall hangings can be displayed in creative and contemporary ways. Use small shelves to float objects like ceramics or even beautiful shoes mid-wall.

* Dried and faux floral displays, wreaths and wall-hung panels make a gentler impact. There are some seriously talented florists creating these currently.

* Vintage shop signs are a bold and quirky choice and easily found online second-hand. It's fun finding one that relates to your own family or interests.

* I'm a big fan of mirrors and sometimes the best picture in your room is a reflection – especially if it is framing a beautiful view of the garden or a characterful corner.

* Don't discount anything that hangs from your walls as both decoration and art – that goes for curtains/blinds and wall lighting – both are excellent opportunities for bringing something special to the room.

Displaying Art Like a Pro
Any artwork can work twice as hard by being properly presented. Professional framing makes a huge difference but even when DIY-ing, taking the time to really consider how to best display your piece will really elevate it. Getting creative with how you hang art in your home and learning how to layer it will make the most out of the art you own.

I often have collections of artworks stacked on shelves or tables – they're easily changeable and I like the artistic feel they have displayed in this relaxed way.

Framing Matters

In the same way we might choose make-up to emphasise our eyes, the right frame can make a picture pop. A good framer will take the time with you to try out lots of combinations to find what makes the most of both the artwork *and* the setting it will be in. If professional framing isn't in the budget, you can still make a choice, either with ready-made frames, second-hand frames or getting the paint test pots out. Just the simple act of comparing a white frame with a black frame for each piece will make a huge difference.

Walls Matter

Always consider what goes behind a picture. Think of a great art gallery and how the wall colours they have chosen become almost as important to the exhibition as the art itself. You don't even need to paint the whole wall, you can paint a shape, like a square or an arch behind the picture or pictures which will visually make the artwork much bigger than it is and draw focus to it. This is especially great for special pieces that you want to make a centrepiece, but are a bit too small to fill the spot you want them in.

Layer it up

I'm a big fan of artwork hung on top of wallpaper. Often there is this belief that you're hiding the wallpaper by putting art on top of it (which can be true if you don't like your wallpaper), but the richness you get from layering a beautiful painting on top of a great wallpaper is just *chef's kiss*. Give it a try!

One of my favourite ways to display art is to hang it on the back of bookshelves and then style it as a small vignette surrounded by books, vases and ornaments.

I also love a good frame stack on the floor or on a shelf – propping larger pieces at the back

with smaller pieces resting in front (see opposite). Layering art is a maximalist's dream and such an easy way to change up a look as often as you like. It is also a brilliant way to tell stories in the way you combine them. Perhaps you're telling the story of how a love of food runs in your family by putting a black and white photo of your grandmother beside a poster of pasta, and a framed menu from your wedding day? Together these pieces tell a bigger story about who you are and what you hold dear.

A Practical Note

If you can use proper hooks on your walls – please do. It will save you a world of pain in the future. If you need to use sticky hooks, get the largest ones you can, press them on super well and leave overnight before hanging your art. Lessen the weight of frames by removing the glass if they're pieces you're not too precious about.

Objects are Art

We've discussed this already, but art is more than what fits in a frame or hangs on the wall. Ceramics, glass, ornaments, sculpture, books, even plants can function as art in the home. It's all about how you display them. If you have a beautiful vase collection, consider installing a shelf where you can make them a feature. Paint the wall behind it to really show them off.

Art is for Everywhere

There is a type of art for every room, even kitchens and bathrooms which are so often overlooked. If you're worried about moisture or heat in these areas, consider things like decorative trays or plates hung on the wall, or low-cost pieces like cool posters. They'll last longer than you think and will bring you a lot of joy while you have them up.

For a bit of fun, I pinned
this beach towel on the
wall above our bed.

BUYING ART

Supporting living artists is a thrill and a delight. And while I do believe everything can be art, there is something so special about buying art from an artist if you can. I feel like I'm just coming into my art-buying era and it's what I'm most excited about. Social media is a brilliant way to find artists and buy pieces from them directly – I recommend signing up to newsletters of artists you love to be first to know when they release new work or exhibit.

Buying art is not just a matter of decorating your space, but investing in pieces that resonate with you personally. Here are some tips to guide you through the process:

1 Follow Your Heart
Most importantly (and this applies to everything, not just art) buy what you love. Art should evoke emotion and add personal value to your space. If a piece catches your eye and you keep thinking about it, that's a good sign it belongs with you. Remember, you're the one who will live with the art, so it should speak to you on a personal level.

2 Set a Budget
Art can range from surprisingly affordable to significantly pricey. Setting a budget before you start looking can help narrow down your options and keep your spending in check. Remember, there are gems at every price point, and starting an art collection doesn't necessarily mean breaking the bank.

3 Educate Yourself
Spend some time learning about different art forms, styles and artists. Visit galleries, art fairs and museum exhibitions to get a sense of what appeals to you. The more you know, the more confident you'll feel in your art-buying decisions.

4 Consider the Space
Think about where the art will go in your home. Consider the size, colour scheme and lighting of the space. Art can be a focal point or complement your existing décor. Sometimes, envisioning where a piece will hang or stand can help solidify your decision to purchase it, especially if it's an investment. Some galleries and artists, especially online, can digitally mock up how an artwork would sit in your space which can be super helpful.

5 Support Emerging Artists
Buying from emerging artists not only helps support their careers but can also be a way to acquire original works at more accessible prices. Plus, there's something special about discovering and nurturing new talent. Keep an eye on local art schools' graduate shows, small galleries and online platforms that showcase up-and-comers.

6 Ask Questions
When buying art, don't hesitate to ask the seller or artist questions. Learn about the piece's story, the materials used, the artist's

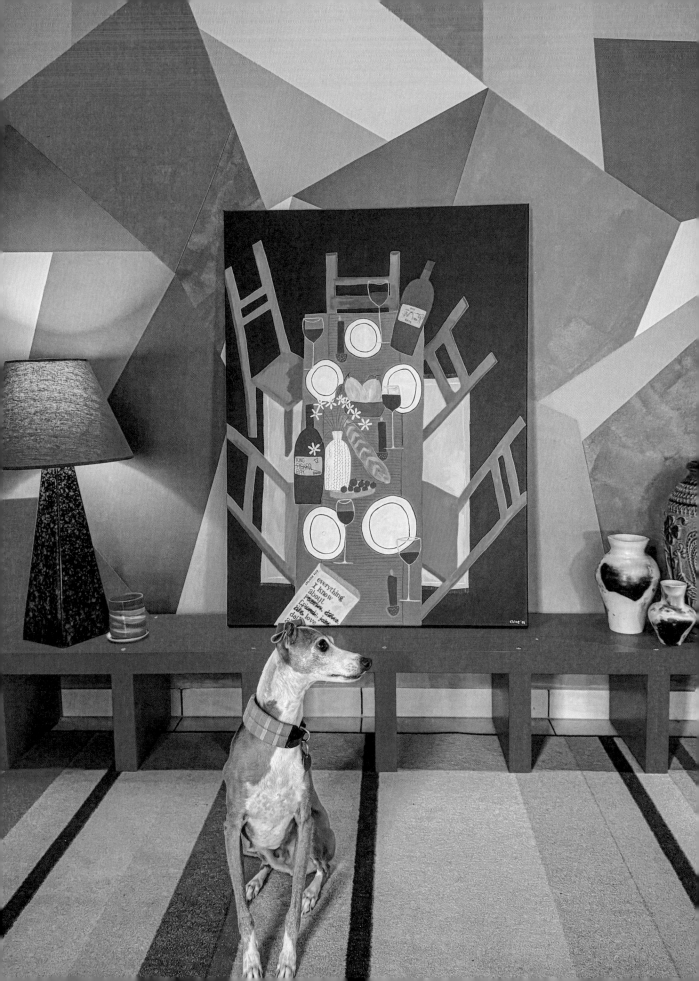

I never stick to just prints or paintings; on this wall I have wooden sculptures, framed postcards and even a framed handkerchief.

background, and the care instructions. This information can add value to the artwork and deepen your connection to it. Artists and gallerists love to talk about art, so never think that you're wasting their time asking questions.

7 Buying Art Online

The internet has made art more accessible than ever. Online galleries, social media platforms and artist websites are great places to discover art from around the world. Just be sure to verify the site's credibility and understand the return policy before making a purchase. Many artists do studio sales via social media – often these will be more affordable pieces like sketches or artist's proofs. This is such a fun way to buy art directly from an artist.

I once enquired about a painting from a Dutch artist I had discovered through Instagram and loved his work. The painting was out of my budget but the artist very kindly let me know that he had a collection of art cards coming out soon as a collaboration and I was delighted to buy them! I'm still hoping to buy an original one day. If I hadn't asked about the painting – which I was shy to given I guessed it would be more than I could afford – I would never have known about the prints which I still treasure today. This is a sign to engage with artists you love, even if you're not necessarily in the market right now.

8 Think Long Term

Consider how the art will grow with you as your taste may evolve, and your living situation

might change. Art that has a timeless appeal or carries personal significance is likely to remain a cherished part of your collection, whereas art bought predominantly as décor or because it fits a colour scheme will probably fail.

9 Enjoy the Process

Art collecting should be enjoyable. Each piece you choose is a reflection of your journey, tastes and experiences. Enjoy the process of searching, discovering and selecting pieces that move you. Don't allow yourself to get stressed or pressured into finding the perfect piece. If you've got a gap on the wall, stick something else up in the meantime like a nicely framed print – the right artwork will find you eventually.

If you're new to collecting and worried that the art scene can be intimidating, don't be. Start popping into galleries and having a good look. It's usually pretty easy to see which ones are more open and accessible, so if you're nervous start with those, or at a student exhibition. Artists want to sell art – you'll be more than welcome, I promise you.

GALLERY WALLS

There are a billion how-to guides for gallery walls across the internet that would have you planning your wall with military precision. I'm much more fond of a relaxed execution that serves the purpose of primarily displaying my favourite things rather than being a test of my maths skills. See overleaf for some key arranging tips.

Top tips for arranging a gallery wall

*

I start every gallery wall by picking my most favourite pieces, deciding where I want them to go and then filling in the gaps.

*

Keep in mind spacing and proportion, without getting too hung up on it. For this wall I knew I wanted to keep the neon sign in the centre and build around it.

*

Hang the largest and most important pieces first and then work backwards to fill in the gaps. I often end up with empty spaces that I get creative with which I enjoy letting evolve over time as I collect more pieces. By starting in the middle and working outwards, you can grow your gallery wall gradually.

*

You can create a cohesive, united gallery wall (if you want) by collecting around a theme (dogs!), by framing (for example only white frames), or a particular colour palette. Alternatively, just do whatever you want!

In the same way we might choose make-up to emphasise our eyes, the right frame can make a picture pop.

Can You Frame Your Own Art?

Of course you can. Can you frame professionally at home? No. Is professional always best? Generally, yes. But framing can be expensive and if budget is limited, save professional framing for special pieces or pieces that need to be preserved.

The most important thing with framing is making sure you have the correct sized frame – or more specifically, the correctly proportioned frame. There are so many different styles of framing – ornate, simple, modern, colourful, rustic. Don't default to a standard black or white frame. Expert framers know how to really enhance an artwork with framing and it's good to consider how a frame can change how the artwork looks.

I don't like to think there are any great rules with framing; often it's about choosing a frame that is similar to the artwork, but sometimes it's creating a great juxtaposition – a modern abstract in a hand-carved gilt frame can look seriously cool.

Second-hand shops are a great source for frames. Sometimes it can take a bit of collecting or hunting to find the right size/style match but when you do, it completely elevates the artwork. I also like to keep an eye out for frames with nice condition coloured mats (the cardboard border inside some frames) that I might use with a different frame.

Mats are a really fun part of framing – they come in all sorts of colours and you have your artwork floating on top, or underneath. Professional framers can do really clever things with them, like a double or even triple colour. You can use mat size to really emphasise a certain colour in the artwork, or increase the size of a piece to make more of a statement.

Many framing supply places will also sell pre-cut mats as well as ready-made frames.

There's a real move towards frames as a continuation of the art, and hand-decorating frames is an easy way to really make a unique piece. I've got a DIY project for this on page 234 for you to give it a try!

Framing at Home

1 Make sure your frame is the correct size for your artwork.

2 Open up the frame by prising back the metal tabs using a butter knife. Remove the backboard and give the glass a thorough clean with a streak-free glass cleaner, in and out. Finish with wiping with a clean, lint-free cloth.

3 Put your artwork in the frame – you can use washi or paper tape to attach to the back of a mat if you're using one.

4 Check that your artwork is straight within the frame.

5 Double- and then triple-check for any specks of dust or marks that escaped your clean. It's so frustrating to have to take the frame apart because you spotted a rogue cat hair!

6 Put the backboard back in place – check the front again – and bend back the tabs using a knife.

7 I like to tape over the edges at the back to seal the frame slightly more against dust.

8 Attach a hanger at the back if it doesn't already have one. Two eyehooks with a string or wire are always easier to hang than a single hook – just make sure they're level and that you're using a nice taut (not stretchy) cord (again, framing supply places often sell little kits of these).

9 Don't put your hanger too close to the top of the frame, or it might show when hooked on the wall.

CHAPTER EIGHT

Styling

My own arrangements can be quite random and just things that I like or make me smile. I love using beautiful books as a base for objects.

NO ONE WAS BORN BEING ABLE TO PUT TOGETHER A BEAUTIFUL VIGNETTE, NO MATTER WHAT THEY TELL YOU.

tyling is learned and practised, and through that, perfected. It's also completely personal and entirely subjective – so go for it.

There are things that make items sing when arranged together or in a certain way, but again the way we see beauty is individual so you can take inspiration from how others style their house, but ultimately, you'll do it your own way.

What is Styling Really?

Styling, in the context of interior design and home décor, is the art of curating and arranging objects within a space to enhance its aesthetic appeal, functionality, and overall atmosphere. It involves selecting and placing furniture, accessories, art, and other decorative items in a way that reflects personal taste; it creates cohesion and adds interest and personality to the home. Think of a house where

it's just plain furniture and nothing else, then think of adding in some plants, cushions, rugs and art – that house has been styled.

Styling is not just about making a space look attractive; it's about telling a story and creating an environment that resonates with the people who live there. It's a thoughtful process that considers the balance of colours, textures, shapes and sizes, as well as the interplay between objects and the space they occupy. It's the fun bit of everything we've talked about so far – bringing all of our lovely things together.

Good styling pays attention to details. It finds the perfect spot for a cherished piece of art, arranges pillows and throws for both comfort and visual appeal, and uses lighting to create the desired mood. It's about creating layers and depth, combining old with new, and mixing textures and patterns to achieve a space that feels collected and lived in.

Styling is dynamic. You're allowed to experiment and change – in fact I encourage it! Shuffling the cushions, or rearranging a shelf is a calming activity for me and it keeps things fresh. You can adapt your space to your evolving tastes, needs, and the seasons. Whether it's setting up a bookshelf, designing a gallery wall, or arranging a coffee table, styling is the finishing touch that transforms a house into a home.

Creating a sense of unity throughout your home

We can put too much emphasis on each room in a house feeling like it matches the rest. Yes, most of us probably don't want to feel like we're stepping into different-themed motel rooms with every door we open, but the chances of that being what your home feels like is really unlikely. If you are staying true to your own likes and dislikes and have defined your own style, you'll feel like you can flex how you design and style different rooms and feel like they all still belong.

There's a concept in interior design known as the 'red thread', a metaphorical thread that ties everything together. It's subtle, a special something that links your spaces together, making your whole home feel like it's in harmony. Think of it as the secret ingredient that gives your design a sense of continuity and flow. This could be anything from a splash of colour that pops up where you least expect it, to a material like oak or brass that makes a recurring cameo throughout your home; or even a design vibe that whispers its way through each room.

It's like having a subtle theme or an inside joke that only your home is in on, threading through each area, whether it's a particular pattern dancing on various textiles and wallpapers, or a recurring motif that makes a gentle nod from room to room. And it's not just about looks, it's about crafting a story, a vibe that's uniquely you, echoing across your living spaces.

By weaving this 'red thread' through your home, you're not just decorating – you are creating a narrative that ties your spaces together in a way that's visually pleasing and deeply personal. It's your design fingerprint, making your house unmistakably yours, seamlessly connecting different areas without them having to shout over each other to be heard. It's clever, it's subtle, and oh-so-satisfying when you see it all come together.

If you feel like a certain room is disconnected from the rest, have a think about what your red thread (or threads) might be and how you could tie that through. In my house I have a few red threads running, one being animal (particularly dog) motifs – you'll spot them in every room in the house. Stripes would be another, and a couple of colours that repeat through for me would be yellow and orange. I don't overly think about these as they're just things I really like, so they end up in almost every room.

Styling with Plants

In recent years we've grown a much better understanding of biophilic design – that being the connection to nature we create in our built environments. Basically, having plants in your house alongside more natural materials, and optimising sunlight. Humans have always loved nature (though they don't always behave as such) and having house plants is nothing new (the Victorians loved a parlour palm), but they do tend to come in and out of fashion.

Dying plants look awful and throwing away dead ones is a downer. I'm all for setting yourself up for success here.

Styling is not just about making a space look attractive; it's about telling a story and creating an environment that resonates with the people who live there.

My Italian greyhound, Biggie, is my
ultimate accessory, even when he
falls asleep on the job. We both
love a good handmade rug.

The principle of biophilic design is that it makes us feel better. That being more in touch with nature impacts our wellbeing, mental and physical health. It's a lot more than a token peace lily in the bathroom, but that is a start.

A crucial point to make is that plants really come down to some of the first things we talked about – making a space that works for how you actually, and want to, live. If you're a green-thumbed goddess, chances are you already have plenty of indoor plants, but for those of us that are more botanically challenged it is good to temper those aspirations. Dying plants look awful and throwing away dead ones is a downer. I'm all for setting yourself up for success here.

I'm someone who loves living with plants so long as they take basically no care and attention. The minute they start looking sad or get a bug infestation I shove them outside (I know, so harsh). But over the years I've really narrowed down the varieties that seem to thrive under my 'care', which is why you'll see mostly rubber trees (Ficus and Dracaenas) indoors here. It's not that they are my most favourite house plants (well, they are now as they are the last plants standing), but that they look healthy and are hard for me to kill. A lush live plant beats a sad one any day. Anything more demanding needs to live in the kitchen, near a water source so I don't forget about it (still not guaranteed).

Plant purists love to turn their noses up at faux greenery, but there are some great artificial plants available and for certain homes, or spots in homes, they are the best solution. So don't be shamed into not buying one if it's what you want! A trick I picked up from my mum (who is very green-thumbed) is mixing faux with real. You see one real plant and your brain fills in the gaps and reads them all as real, meaning you can have a bit more variety with less lives in your hands. Dark corners or bright sunspots are difficult places for real plants, so have live plants in the appropriate spot and stick a faux palm in that dark corner if you fancy.

Personal preference plays a big part in styling your home with plants – you'll see incredible rooms just absolutely packed with plants while most homes have just one or two. Personally, I like bigger plants that add a bit of architecture to the place (also give me one big plant to care for over 10 small ones any day!).

My most impressive plant – the big rubber tree in my living room – has a bit of a funny story as to how it came to be in my possession. When I was young and ignorant and searching online for fake plants, I was trying all the words I could think of: 'faux', 'fake', 'artificial', 'plastic' and then I searched 'rubber plant' ... yep. It just didn't click to me that they were real trees. So I found this decent-sized 'rubber plant' and thought it was a bargain! When I picked it up, I was surprised to find there was real soil in the pot and that it was in fact a real, live tree that I needed to care for. Against all odds it has thrived and I'm very fond of it (we've been together a really long time). Confession though – and this is going to horrify some people – I've never repotted it.

My favourite way to use plants is to soften a room. A trailing plant from a shelf or bookcase can bring an organic nature to what otherwise is a lot of straight lines. They're also great for filling dead space – creating interesting shapes and texture to corners or awkward spots.

The pots and planters you use are also key pieces of décor. A bit like a lampshade on a lamp, you want to get the proportions right first and then think about material, style and colour. Does your room suit grey concrete planters? Fresh white? Or more of an eclectic mix with lots of terracotta? You can of course paint your own pots too!

Shelves, bookcases, sideboards and coffee tables
Now this really is my favourite thing about making a home. Finding a place for all my lovely things and making them really sing. Rearranging a shelf or a table is just so satisfying. A big part of the fun of bringing home a new vase or cushion is how you can use it as an opportunity to reimagine a corner of your home.

Beyond aesthetics, styling your home is about creating comfort and functionality, designing spaces that not only look beautiful but also cater to your lifestyle and wellbeing. It's about the pleasure of curling up in a cosy nook you've created, making room for the things that matter most, and the sense of belonging in a space that's uniquely yours.

Moreover, styling your home is an ongoing process, not a destination. It grows and changes as you do, adapting to new trends, experiences and phases of life. There's joy in the flexibility and freedom to reinvent your environment, to keep adding layers that tell new stories, and to continuously create a home that feels right for you at any given moment.

The joy also comes from the challenge – the problem-solving aspect of making the most of your space, whether it's finding clever storage solutions, creating multipurpose areas, or bringing light and warmth into a previously dull corner. It's about the triumphs, big and small, from creating a functional kitchen that displays your full collection of retro dinnerware, to making your bedside table a little moment of calm.

Here are a few pointers to keep in mind when styling: I hate rules so these aren't hard and fast, rather some gentle guides to assist you as you practise and gain confidence. You'll soon have the eye for it. The more confident you are the more you're able to break the rules.

✳ Style in odd-numbered groups. For example, start with three vases. The asymmetry of the odd number makes it seem less contrived and more organic, which our brains like.

✳ Vary heights and combine short, medium and tall. This leads our eye to move over the scene, rather than reading it as one solid block.

✳ Add height and texture by using books or trays to elevate smaller items. These also help anchor a

Fusing organic and geometric shapes brings together the raw elegance of nature with the structured, deliberate creations of human hands.

Juxtapose textures like glossy and matte, or rough and smooth.

scene which instantly makes it seem more intentional – 'displaying' an object rather than just 'placing' it. Negative space is an important element in styling too, and how much of it you want is personal preference so play around with different spacings and see what feels most right to you. This is where using different heights really helps to create this balance.

* Is there an echo, echo, echo in here? There should be. Echo across colours, themes and even shapes from the whole room. You can make tiny little echoes that will make a room hang together without being glaringly obvious. Look around the room right now – do you see any echoed elements that are helping to pull your space together?

* It all comes back to layers. If you're styling in front of a wall, consider layering a picture behind your vignette. If styling a coffee table, make sure it has focal points from any side. Instagram has made us a bit partial to a good angle, and while it might make a nice photo, remember that in real life we see things from all angles.

* Combine organic and geometric forms to create interest. Fusing organic and geometric shapes brings together the raw elegance of nature with the structured, deliberate creations of human hands. It's this blend, this conversation, that infuses a room with complexity and fascination. An example of this could be a boxy, mirrored side table paired with flowers in

a wobbly handmade vase – the friction between the shapes and textures makes it interesting and instantly appealing, but also balances it out.

* On a similar note, juxtapose textures like glossy and matte, or rough and smooth.

* Don't stick to one era – putting old and new together makes your collections look genuine and less like a catalogue or showroom. Merging pieces from various time periods allows for the expression of individual taste and personality. It results in a unique aesthetic that can't be replicated. It adds layers of visual and historical depth to a space. Each piece carries its own story, its design influenced by the cultural, social and technological context of its time. This blend not only creates visual interest but also invites curiosity and conversation about the origins and histories of the items. It's also the key to creating a timeless home, because an interior that encompasses a range of design movements is inherently flexible. It allows for the introduction of new pieces or the reconfiguration of existing ones without being tied down to a specific style. This versatility makes it easier to update your space or incorporate new finds and favourites over time.

* While a colour palette is a brilliant and vital way to define your space, be loose with it when styling and add in some wild cards and tones to keep it exciting. These spontaneous pops of colour can draw the eye,

Clockwise from left: I can't help but love a bit of retro, especially when it comes in yellow; play around with where things can go, few things are permanent – this poster is now hung in our hallway but I enjoyed it here for a few months; this charming metal doll's house serves as a practical storage unit in our kitchen.

break up monotony, and add layers of complexity to the design. I love a yellow, or a zingy green for this, but bright red is also a fun addition. Using colour in this way helps loosen up our style, and through that brings more authenticity.

✳ Be quirky, go back to your storytelling and don't shy away from sharing the weird and wonderful things you own. I have some super weird stuff in my house, and rather than hiding it away I display it loud and proud. The metal doll's house I have in my kitchen serves as a small cupboard for all that kitchen bench junk (bills, cables, library cards) and I bought it because I was so charmed by it. It might (probably does) seem pretty odd for someone to have a doll's house in their kitchen, but it is where my passion for all this began, and I'm still completely fascinated by anything miniature, so why not? The fact that it has a very practical purpose tickles me, and I love how often I get to say, 'It's in the doll's house!'

✳ When styling on a shelf or sideboard, try styling asymmetrically by drawing the eye over to one side, rather than defaulting to the centre. This works because it's how we see beauty in nature – like a tree that frames a view, rigid symmetry lacks that organic feel that we're drawn to. When styling multiple shelves, try shifting the focal point on each so that your eye reads across, up and down – almost like a piece of sheet music.

✳ A stylist addeth and a stylist taketh away: bundle together as many bits and pieces as you can to switch and swap with. I always end up with gaps where I've pinched pieces from other rooms to restyle another. It's a never-ending game. There are infinite possibilities for how you can style your house and it should be fun.

Take an hour to style a shelf, sideboard or small table in your home. Start by completely clearing it of everything and then try and style it in a few different ways, taking photos as you go so you can see what you liked the most.

If you can style a shelf, you can style anything. The same principles apply when styling a whole room – levels, layers, echoes, texture. The only limit is your confidence, which you hopefully have buckets of!

DRESSING THE BED

Styling a bed might seem like a whole different kettle of fish compared to arranging objects on a bookshelf, but it really shares most of the same principles. Consider height, colour, texture, mixing pattern and creating layers. How full you want your bed to look, and feel, is again up to you. Think of a bed you've slept in that felt luxurious – how can you emulate this at home and within your own style?

Start with a Solid Foundation

Begin with quality bedding that feels sumptuous – think high-thread-count cotton or linen. I personally like cotton for my fitted sheet and then either cotton or linen on top, the reason being that as a restless sleeper I find linen stretches and tangles as a fitted sheet. Good-quality bedding is almost always an investment, but it's an item that you really do get what you pay for. I love brands like Sage and Clare, Bed Threads and Society of Wanderers for beautiful bedding that will stand the test of time.

Be quirky, go back to your story-telling and don't shy away from sharing the weird and wonderful things you own.

Our guest bedroom is small, so I like to layer it up with lots of wonderful fabrics to make it feel really warm and welcoming. Maeby (the cat) agrees.

Layer for Texture and Depth

I like a top sheet, and then a duvet with either a plain or patterned cover. On top of that I often have a comforter or blanket that I have folded down on the bottom half of the bed. It visually breaks up the expanse of the duvet but is also there ready to be pulled up in the night if it gets chilly.

Pile on the Pillows

Pillows add personality and comfort. Start with a set of sleeping pillows with pillowcases that you want to actually sleep on; again I avoid linen here because I end up with too many lines on my face. From there I'll add a second pillow, usually with a more decorative pillowcase. Behind those I'll have Euro pillows for height and back support when reading in bed.

Then I add on the extras – the decorative cushions that I'll throw on in the morning that really serve very little purpose other than to make the bed look lovely and inviting. It takes me about 10 seconds to throw these cushions on the floor and another 10 seconds to put them back on when I make the bed in the morning. These are a really fun opportunity to mix patterns with solids and add in different colours or patterns. This is where your bed gets its character.

Accentuate with a Throw

A throw blanket at the bed's foot brings in texture, colour, and an element of casual elegance. Choose a throw that complements your colour scheme but feel free to play with contrasting textures – chunky knits, smooth cashmere, or even a touch of fringe can add visual and tactile interest.

Consider the Surroundings

The bed is the focal point, but the rest of the room is all part of how it feels. Bedside tables, lighting and wall art should work harmoniously with the feeling you're trying to create in the room. Symmetry in bedside tables and lamps can create a balanced look, while a statement piece of art above the bed or a fabulous headboard can draw the eye upward, adding dimension to the space.

A note on bedroom art: there has long been an opinion that a bedroom needs to be extremely tranquil, but a bold artwork above the bed doesn't conflict that. When you're sitting or lying in bed you can't see it!

Don't Forget the Senses

Lighting is so important in a bedroom and having lamps is non-negotiable. I really recommend dimmable light bulbs for in here; the less light (and fewer screens) the better your sleep will be. You can also think about scent, having a candle you light before bed, or a diffuser. Clean linen and even a lavender pillow spray can feel so luxurious.

Personal Touches

Finally, infuse your styled bed with elements that are uniquely you. Whether it's a vintage throw picked up on travels, a beloved book placed on the bedside table, or a cherished photograph on the wall, these personal touches make the space feel intimately yours. This really is your inner sanctum, so get selfish with how it looks and feels in here.

CHAPTER NINE

Sourcing

Ceramic dogs are not
something I need, but how
could I leave this little pink
poodle behind?

MY MUM IS MY BIGGEST INSPIRATION, HELPER AND CHEERLEADER.

She's also the greatest second-hand shopper I've ever known. In 2016, Mum proved it, buying a second-hand conservatory for the house for $500 and winning NZ Interior of the Year!

For most of my childhood, my dad was a student and there were five of us kids, so almost everything was second-hand by necessity. At primary school I was teased and ashamed when other kids recognised that I was wearing second-hand clothes, and all I ever wanted was new stuff. This isn't to evoke pity; we never went without and had many lovely things – I just found it hard to appreciate. We were always different, and in a small village in the early nineties, that difference seemed magnified. I love seeing my friends' kids now who love thrifting. The stigma seems to be on buying fast fashion, not second-hand – which makes a lot more sense to me.

Despite complaining a lot about just wanting a new pair of Reeboks, I actually loved trawling around charity shops and car boot sales with my mum and siblings, looking for treasure. *Antiques Roadshow* and *Bargain Hunt* were some of my favourite TV programmes even when I was little, and I liked the opportunity to test my knowledge – unsuccessfully, I might add.

I'm not sure my mum has ever really tried to fit in. She's always the most glamorous person in the room and infinitely creative with everything – her personal style, her cooking, her garden and of course, her home. For her, choosing to buy second-hand is a way to ensure things are unique and special; one of a kind is even better. I like to think the best thing I've inherited from my mum is her can-do attitude and seeing budget as an inspiration, not a limitation.

Thrift shopping is still a go-to activity for my family, and I'll hit the second-hand shops with my mum and sisters, Lily and Grace, at least once a month. Thankfully it's less competitive than it used to be as we've each grown into our own styles, but we have been known to have public arguments over who saw something first (I'm the eldest so obviously it was me!).

Second-hand shopping is my most favourite thing: the challenge of the hunt, the thrill of the find, the satisfaction of a bargain. It's not all wins though, and accepting that is a big part of the game.

In this chapter I'm going to share how to find and buy great home pieces second-hand, as well as a few other notes on sourcing in general. If you're new to buying second-hand and feel a bit weird about it – don't. It's the same as having a piece of furniture that has been passed down through your family, or given to you by a friend; the only difference is that you've chosen and paid for it.

Honestly, this could (and perhaps should!?) be a whole book in itself, but I wanted to share a couple of my main tips for second-hand success!

∗ I don't believe buying second-hand is exclusively for antiques. It's a great way to buy newer, lightly used items you might not normally be able to afford. I've only bought a brand-new sofa once in my whole life, and it was a huge mistake. It wasn't an especially cheap one by any standards, but within months the upholstery was bobbled and worn. I managed to get a partial refund from where I had bought it and used that towards having it reupholstered (it's the grey leopard-print sofa you might spot in some photos). I loved it once it was reupholstered but the upholstery plus the price of a brand-new sofa made it a really expensive project. I could have bought a better-quality piece of furniture for a quarter (or less) of the price and then invested in having that covered instead. Lesson learnt.

∗ There's no quick way to really go about it. I scroll online sale sites pretty much every day. Here in New Zealand that's Trade Me and Facebook Marketplace, but could be eBay and the likes for others. I also go to charity shops and markets whenever I can. Chances are you have a friend who is all over the online second-hand offerings; let them know what you're looking for and I promise you'll have daily listings sent direct to your inbox (we can't help it, it's that thrill of the hunt!).

∗ Don't search just with keywords. Everyone describes things differently and typos are rife! If I'm looking for cool chairs, I will trawl all possible chair categories on a website. I'll then search by general words to find any miscategorised items. No stone is left unturned!

∗ Always look at the listings with terrible photos. I've found some incredible bargains because of a blurry garage shot other people weren't willing to take a risk on. One of my most favourite examples of this is my long 1970s couch which I bought for $100. The photos were so terrible, you really couldn't get much of an idea about it other than the red covers were filthy. I could see it had a great shape though, and was intrigued enough to bid. I picked it up and immediately knew it was something special – it has zebrawood veneer and bookshelves in the armrests. Another reupholstery job, but this time it cost me a lot less and I ended up with a much higher-quality piece of furniture.

∗ Quality is everything; if a brand is a bit shonky new, it will be ten times more so when it's already been used, so if you can pay a bit more to buy quality, it's so worth it in the long run. And it will have resale value should you change your mind! You'll know the type of brands I'm talking about according to what stores you have available – pieces that won't last five years will have even less left on the clock if you're buying them used.

You really don't need to be an expert to be able to make a basic call on something if it is well made. Trust yourself with this.

Clockwise from top right: Second-hand shopping is a great way to try out styles without spending lots of money – this Arts and Crafts footstool was a nice addition for a couple of years but now belongs to my mum; some pieces come back around so while this chrome glass table is currently stored in the garage, I'm holding on to it because I know I'll use it again; you just never know what you're going to find – this terrarium lamp was found filled with gravel, small ceramic figurines and artificial succulents at a local charity shop.

* If you're looking for a project to reupholster or fix up, overlook superficial flaws and focus on shape and good bones! It has to stand the test of time to make both the cost and the time worth it. When assessing quality, look for things like solid wood, feather cushions, how the joints are constructed, and sturdiness. You really don't need to be an expert to be able to make a basic call on something if it is well made. Trust yourself with this.

* Similarly, don't delude yourself with what you're actually willing, and able, to do. Upholstery is fabulous but it can be very expensive. I'm the first person to hold my hands up and admit to being guilty of bringing home a project piece of furniture with no real budget or idea of how I'll bring it back to life. I try and keep in mind what I'm willing and able to do myself, and if that's possible, do I really want to do it? Sometimes yes, sometimes no!

* Do your research. If you're not sure on what your budget should be, or you've spotted something you love but you're not convinced it's a fair price, do a Google search – a reverse image search can be great for this.

* Be patient. The perfect piece at the perfect price might not appear immediately. Frequent visits to your favourite second-hand shops or regular checks on online marketplaces increase your chances of finding great deals. The right thing will come along, sometimes you just have to be patient! And sometimes you just get lucky.

* For this stripy armchair (page 201) I had a really specific wish of the type of armchair I wanted – one that looked like it was constructed from pillows (*extremely* specific). I honestly thought there was no way I'd find that, but I was willing to consider any big squishy chair. On my first look online, I found this chair for $150 and I already had the fabric ready to go. I rarely get quite that lucky, but also if you just keep looking, things come up!

* Measure twice. This might seem so obvious, but when checking measurements, it's worth not only checking that the thing you're buying actually fits in the space it's intended for, but that it will also fit through the door, or up a narrow staircase if that's where it's going. I think we can all picture that nightmare of a piece of furniture stuck halfway up the stairs, only for it to go no further but have damaged the wall in the process. And if you have to hire a van or have it paid to be delivered, are you still okay with the price?

* Keep an open mind. Some of my favourite pieces were not at all what I was originally looking for, but when I considered them as possibilities, they were a better solution than I had in mind. This goes back to how you search for things if you're looking online. For example, you might have it in your head that you are a looking for a coffee table, but then you find an amazing ottoman and realise that with a tray on top it's a far better solution for a smaller lounge. Not being able to find the exact piece you are picturing can sometimes be a wonderful thing.

Quality furniture for outdoors is an absolute must or it just won't last. I like to personalise simpler pieces with bright textiles.

* A note on online auctions. If you really love something (as you should if you're going to buy it!), and it has a 'Buy Now' price that seems fair and within your budget, buy it immediately to secure it. Don't risk the heartbreak of losing the auction or missing the closing time!

* Accept your losses. There are always going to be things that turn out to be disappointing. It really is a game of 'you win some you lose some'. Be a good loser and responsibly dispose of the things that didn't work out. Don't dump broken items at charity shops as they have to pay to dispose of them. Offer them for free in your community or pay to dispose of them, if they're not donatable.

* Keep your thrifting karma positive! Donate great stuff to your favourite charities from time to time. Remember the thrill you get from finding treasure and share some of that forward. I have no definitive proof of the thrifting karma, but I believe it to be a powerful force! It's also just really nice to know that something will find a new home, with someone who is thrilled to have found it, and you have helped raise funds for a worthy cause. And don't forget you've given yourself an opportunity to do a spot of shopping while you're there.

* If you find yourself getting a bit carried away with the sheer amount of amazing things you're finding (we've all been there), put some rules in place – maybe it's a 'one in, one out' policy, or being strict on only buying what you actually need and making sure everything you bring home is either needed or deeply desired.

* Rome (and home) weren't built in a day. It can take a while to build up a collection, but enjoy the evolution, and enjoy the hunt!

Buying at Auction

I don't mean buying at Sotheby's, but at your local auction houses (though if you're in the market for Sotheby's – go nuts). I believe that great bargains can still be had at traditional auctions, more so than on big sites. There is generally a smaller pool of people looking, and the types of things that go to general auction are often from either deceased estates or lots from people who can afford to send it to auction rather than selling independently. Auction houses also often screen what is coming through the sale, as they can only have so many lots, which means better-quality, interesting items are more frequent. The established clientele of auction houses are also usually people more interested in art, antiques, design and curios which means that even if nothing catches your fancy this time, it's unlikely to be boring to have a look at. Basically, auctions are great for weirdos, and we're the weirdos!

Like with art dealers, don't be intimidated by auctions. Most now offer online bidding on almost everything, and if it's in person, just be honest and tell a member of staff that it's your first time and ask if they could guide you through it.

Auction pricing can be a bit misleading, as the winning bid (if over the reserve – the reserve being the lowest amount a seller has agreed to sell an item for) will always incur a buyer's premium. This is a percentage that the auction house adds on as their fee. This is generally between 15–25 per cent of the hammer price, plus tax.

Keep these extra costs in mind of your total budget. Real auctions can be exciting and it can be easy to get carried away, so I usually just mentally add 25 per cent to work out what my real top bid can be, and try and stick to that.

Most pieces sold at auction are 'as is, where is' and it is the buyer's responsibility to check they are happy with the condition before placing a bid.

Sometimes buying second-hand means a bit of trial and error – this little retro couch wasn't right for the space but now lives very happily with my friend Anahita.

Auction catalogues for general items and lower-value pieces don't usually have much extra detail beyond dimensions and a very basic description (like *really* basic – 'a metal teapot' for example). If you're able to go along on viewing days and have a look in person, I'd recommend this; and if not, you can request a condition report on particular items and ask any questions you need to.

Etsy

I used to have an Etsy shop, years ago, selling things I'd made, back when it was entirely a handmade online craft market. It's moved away from that a lot in recent years and is no longer as great for small artists and makers as it used to be – there are still so many great shops on there but you often have to already know of them via Instagram to find them. However, I've found it to be an amazing resource for buying textiles from other parts of the world, direct from the source.

On Etsy you'll find tons of authentic Moroccan, Turkish, and Persian rugs – ranging from antique, to second-hand, to made-to-order, at various price points. You can also find beautiful regional fabrics like Ghanaian Kente cloth or Uzbek silk velvets, alongside vintage American quilts or retro Scandinavian cotton canvas. Years ago, back when it was hard to get it here in New Zealand, I would buy short ends and offcuts of Marimekko fabric from a shop based in Finland that I assume was close to the Marimekko outlet. There are also lots of pieces of designer fabrics on there, as well as people making cushions, etcetera from there.

I've bought multiple Moroccan rugs via Etsy with great success, as well as cushions, vintage throws, art and even jewellery (I tend to stay away from breakable items as they have so far to travel). Just check the shop reviews before you purchase, and double-check your measurements!

Buying New

If I give the impression of never buying new, I apologise for misleading you because I absolutely do – I just don't buy *much* new. There are, of course, times that buying new is the best solution for you, either practically for something like a mattress or simply because you've found something you love and you really want it. That's absolutely fine. I'm not here to shame anyone about their choices, especially as I am far from perfect myself. We can all make better choices 90 per cent of the time, but we also need to make choices that make us (and our home) feel good.

Buying new adds an extra layer of consideration for most of us – not only because it might cost more, but because we also assign more weight to how much we really like something, or think we'll use it. These are important things to consider for anything we're bringing into our home, but especially if we're buying new.

When buying new, the same basic principles apply as when buying second-hand: check for quality and try to buy the best quality you can. New things will always look pretty good from the outside, but get a feel for how well made it is; where was it made and what is it made from? Does it feel light and flimsy? I know I sound like Goldilocks, but having to send something to the tip a few years later isn't okay any more. Not for the planet and not for you and your lovely home.

One of the benefits of buying new is having a warranty. Check what it is and know your consumer rights for big purchases.

A Note on Moroccan Rugs
(my absolute favourites)

Shaggy wool rugs like Moroccan berbers and boucherites do tend to have a strong smell when they arrive – they smell quite woolly and can also have lasting smells from the dye. This will quickly fade so don't be alarmed when you open the bag. You can also spritz it with room spray or perfume to eliminate the smell faster. Also, these particular types of rugs do tend to not be entirely colourfast – they have very vibrant colours and no backing. This won't be a problem unless you get them wet – just a warning! And if you are putting this kind of rug on top of existing carpet, I recommend using an underlay.

*

Don't be deterred though; these are traditional rugs made in traditional ways and that's all part of their beauty – we can't expect everything to be entirely sterile, waterproof and have no maintenance if we want the beautiful things. Just be aware of how to care for them properly and they'll bring so much joy.

Rome (and home) weren't built in a day. It can take a while to build up a collection, but enjoy the evolution, and enjoy the hunt!

CHAPTER TEN

Making

In our powder room I painted
the walls, the vanity, the sink,
and even the tap!

SO MUCH OF CREATING A UNIQUE HOME INVOLVES MAKING.

Making a home can be as simple as setting the table for dinner or building the entire structure. DIY and craft are both huge passions of mine. I love the process of making something by hand, the problem solving, and the pride that comes with a job well done – well most of the time anyway. A lot of my projects come from wanting something unique or specific that I can't find to buy – the answer is usually to make it, or modify something. With home improvements it's more from budget and necessity, saving my budget to buy the pretty things I want to add.

If you weren't brought up around DIY it can feel a bit daunting to knock holes into your walls, but there's a reason it's so popular – a lot of it is actually relatively easy and gets easier the more you do. We've already talked about painting your own walls and hanging pictures, but what's stopping you from taking on other tasks around the house? Restoring a piece of wooden furniture can be a really rewarding way to learn some woodworking skills; or tiling a small tabletop can give you a taster of working with tiles before embarking on a bigger project.

Upholstery

Upholstery is my absolute favourite DIY activity. It's something I'm forever challenging myself with to get better at by finding more involved projects and getting stuck in. I'm inspired by my Grandma Gina (my dad's mum) who at 87 is still updating

I love the process of making something by hand, the problem solving, and the pride that comes with a job well done – well most of the time anyway.

her furnishings. My grandma has always been an incredibly resourceful and practical person (thrifty too – there's a theme here). She apparently once repaired the bodywork on her car using gap filler and a net curtain (not something I'll be trying). Always a brilliant sewer and with a head for numbers (I don't think any of us inherited), Grandma has always made the most precise fitted covers for furniture – both her own and for my aunties and mum and dad. I don't think I've ever sat on a chair or sofa with the original fabric, and I try and channel her skills as best I can.

Here are some of my upholstery projects. None of them are perfect but I do think, for the most part, each one is better than the last!

My top tip for learning upholstery (and this applies to any DIY project) is to start with an easy win – a simple project that you know you can achieve a good outcome with and be excited for the finished product. Ideas for this would be the seat on a dining chair, or a small ottoman. Something that's square where the only fiddly bits are the corners (again, YouTube will be your friend here!). Choose a fabric you love so that you're really happy with the finished piece. That will inspire you to keep going.

In the following pages, I've chosen some of my personal favourite projects to really personalise your home.

Painting Murals

Painting a mural can range from a few splodges on the wall, to full Michelangelo – I choose (yes, let's pretend it's a choice) to err more on the splodgy side. Murals can be a cool way to add dimension to a room, or a more affordable way to get the look of wallpaper. The first mural I ever painted was a rainbow stripe across my living room. It still delights me how many murals that simple colour combo inspired – I've even seen manicure art versions of it. It still comes up on my Pinterest feed at least once a week, which goes to show you – murals, even simple ones, make an impact. So, if you feel like a room in your house is lacking a certain sumthin-sumthin, maybe a mural is it.

I can't mention murals without name-dropping the queen of modern interior murals and generous sharer of inspiration and practical tips – Racheal Jackson (@BanyanBridges on Instagram). If you want to get really inspired with your painting, she is the place to start.

If you can't find what you want, make it! This lamp was a fun experimental project using foam tubes and spray paint.

This zebrawood sofa was an absolute bargain for $100 and I've since made a few different sets of covers for it so I can change the look. I've never seen anything else quite like it.

And if you want to be reminded that practice makes perfect as you watch how smoothly she can paint a line, Racheal started painting her home as an outlet for post-natal depression; she now paints murals all over the USA and even has a TV show!

I'm not saying you need to be planning your HGTV special when you pick up the paintbrushes, but I think it's a good reminder of how there might be a passion and a creative calling you haven't even found yet.

Anyway, let's get back to mural painting and a few of my own pieces of advice.

✳ Murals don't have to be huge. You can use a spot or blob of colour behind a shelf or a picture to make more of a feature of it. Or just paint a decorative trim or exaggerate the door frame. They also don't have to be on the walls; ceiling murals can look super fun – just book in a massage for after.

✳ Inspiration for murals is only limited to what you feel you can achieve. If you're already an artist, why not super-size your art? If you like things a bit more ordered, how about a stripe or a check?

✳ You can use as many colours as you like, but some of my favourites are just a single-coloured line on top of a coloured background. For our loo (page 218), I was inspired by the pattern of some Kelly Wearstler

fabric. The style of the design called for painterly brushstrokes which meant it was a single coat and I embraced the brush texture. It made for the quickest paint job ever, but looks great.

✳ My favourite way to plan a mural is to take a photo of the wall/s and draw on top of it on my tablet; you can also print this out and draw or paint on it. Don't get too precise – you'll only make it more difficult for yourself. A loose plan that takes into account the features in the room (such as what will be behind the TV, for example) is something to refer back to as you paint.

✳ If you prefer a tighter plan, either project your design onto the wall or measure out a grid on your plan and wall to help with scale and placement.

✳ Try to avoid drawing on the wall with a pencil. Graphite is surprisingly hard to cover up and you'll find it still shows through a lot of paint colours. If you want to mark your basic design on the wall before committing, I recommend a medium-sized brush with just a little bit of paint on it, so that you can paint a really light guide.

✳ The easiest designs are organic shapes that don't touch. Where two colours meet, you have to make sure one is completely dry before applying the second colour to get a clean edge.

Have fun! Stick a podcast on and take your time. And remember, it's just paint! You can always paint over it.

If you intentionally design with space between shapes, you can paint whatever, whenever and you also give yourself a little bit of flexibility with those edges.

* Don't get hung up on perfection! When you've got your nose right up to that painted edge you can get obsessed with every little wobble. Step back and see the whole picture and it will look a million times better. If you keep trying to correct an area, what usually happens is it just gets bigger and bigger and any mistake becomes more obvious. If you struggle to step away, promise yourself you'll move on for now but allow yourself to look at it again at the end (then just leave it alone, okay?).

* The best way to get a really nice smooth edge, especially on a curve, is by using a good-quality brush (I like to use an angle cutter brush) with a nice load of paint. Not so much paint that you get drips, but enough so that you can do a nice long, smooth stroke with the brush. You'll get a feel for this, and you can see the bead of paint rolling along the edge of the brush as you go. You could get an old piece of board and practise this technique before committing to the walls.

* If you're painting larger shapes, use a small roller to fill in the centre. You don't want your mural to be too thick and blobby (unless texture is what you're looking for) because it will tend to drip before it's completely dry, as well as being a pain to paint over if you eventually want to. If you have thick shapes on top of your wall, it will need sanding back.

* If you're using masking tape, be sure to smooth it down with a credit card or similar and remove it while the paint is still wet if you can. This stops the paint from peeling off with the tape and gives a cleaner edge.

* You'll probably only need sample pots for most murals – they don't take up too much paint. If you can have a brush and roller for each colour, it will be much easier to swap between colours or go back and touch up than if you're washing and drying brushes in between. Keep wet brushes and rollers wrapped in plastic wrap, or in old plastic bags between painting to keep them fresh and stop them drying out – this applies for between coats for regular painting too.

* Have fun! Stick a podcast on and take your time. And remember (I've said it before and I'll say it again, and again), it's just paint! You can always paint over it.

* See overleaf for my top tips when taking on a DIY project of your own.

Top DIY tips

1 Start small. If you're new or daunted by the idea of DIY, start small with something manageable. I'm all about the easy wins to give you confidence.

2 Invest in some tools. You don't need a whole shed load but a few pieces of kit will make life much easier. An electric screwdriver is a must-have for every home in my opinion!

3 Assume you're going to make a mess. It's far quicker to prep for making a mess, than to think you can be careful and then be scrubbing stains out of the carpet later.

4 I always smooth down any masking tape with a plastic card to make sure I get nice, crisp lines. Always peel it off before the paint is completely dry if you can! It will come off much cleaner.

5 Follow product directions – especially drying times. They really are recommended for a reason and you don't want all your hard work going to waste!

6 Measure twice, cut once. Plan your cuts and measurements carefully.

7 YouTube is your friend. Use really specific search terms to find video tutorials of people doing exactly what you want to learn.

8 If at first you don't succeed, try and try again! I find it so empowering when I accomplish something I wasn't sure I could do and it makes me want to do more!

I turned this old tool chest into my beauty product storage unit. It's amazing the difference paint and new handles can make!

See overleaf for the final result...

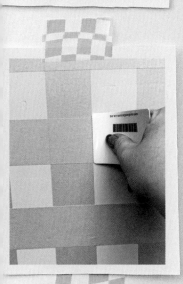

A lot of my projects come from wanting something unique or specific that I can't find to buy — the answer is usually to make it, or modify something.

DIY Project #1

HOW TO COVER A READY-MADE LAMPSHADE

The most affordable way to get a custom lampshade is to cover one you've already got in a gorgeous new fabric. This is a great project to use a really special fabric with, as depending on the size of your shade, you won't need a large amount. Look out for one-of-a-kind fabrics, like a great vintage print or even something with embroidery.

YOU'LL NEED:
* Fabric
* Pre-made drum lampshade
* Spray adhesive suitable for glueing fabrics
* Good-quality double-sided tape
* Scissors
* Measuring tape or ruler
* Drop cloth or sheet or newspaper
* Butter knife or popsicle stick

1 Your existing lampshade should be a drum or cylinder shape, and ideally a light colour so as much light shines through as possible once it's covered.

2 Measure your fabric. The best way to do this is to lay your fabric out flat and put your lampshade on its side on the fabric. Mark where the shade starts (use the existing seam), and mark on your fabric, rolling the shade along until it has completed a revolution. Mark the other end of the fabric, then mark your top and bottom edges.

Add a 1 cm allowance to this. Measure again. The saying 'measure twice, cut once' is a good mantra to have! Cut.

3 Take your shade and fabric outside, or to a well-ventilated area and lay out your drop cloth to collect any overspray. Evenly coat the outside of the lampshade with the spray adhesive (be sure to give it a good shake as per product instructions first), and leave it for 30 seconds or so. You want it to be tacky but not wet. Take care not to apply too much glue or it will soak through your fabric. For larger shades you might want to glue in sections to avoid it drying too quickly.

4 Starting at the seam, carefully smooth your fabric on to the shade. I like to do this by rolling the same way as we measured the fabric. Smooth out any air bubbles with your finger or a credit card. If any areas aren't sticking, pull back and apply a bit more glue.

5 When you get back round to the seam, fold under the edge (you can give this a quick iron) and stick down so that it overlaps the raw edge. Try and get the seam to sit over the existing shade seam so you can position this to the back.

6 Stick a length of double-sided tape along the inside edge of the round wire along the top and bottom of your shade. Fold the fabric over the wire ring and then use a butter knife to carefully tuck in your top and bottom edges around the wire. Press and squeeze on the wire as you go to get

the tape to hold – you could use a hot glue gun for this. If you have too much fabric for this, give it a trim. A good-quality double-sided tape will hold well for years (I swear by tesa 4965 tape), and you'll create extra hold by tucking in the edges of your fabric underneath the edge of the ring.

And there you have it, a completely new lampshade!

DIY Project #2

HAND-PAINTED TABLECLOTH

Painting a tablecloth is a really simple and effective project that is such a pleasure to work on and then to use. It can also make a really nice gift for someone, or is a fun way to theme a party or picnic.

YOU'LL NEED:
* A light-coloured cotton or linen tablecloth (or a hemmed piece of fabric)
* Acrylic paint (or a sample pot of wall paint works too)
* Jar for mixing
* Paintbrush
* Iron
* Drop cloth or old sheet

1 Lay out your drop cloth to protect your table – you may want to iron this to give you a smooth painting surface. Spread your tablecloth over the top. You want to paint from the middle first as it's easiest to see the finished design this way.

2 Mix your paint. Acrylic and house paints have a plastic feel when applied to fabric directly, but with water they soften and soak more into the fabric for a nicer finish. You want to find the balance between being nice to paint with but not so watery that the paint soaks and bleeds through the fabric. Test the consistency on the corner of your drop cloth first.

3 Paint your designs – I chose simplistic dinner motifs like glasses, bowls of pasta, baguettes, etcetera but you can do anything. Don't overthink it – the sketchy quality of the paint strokes is all part of the charm.

4 Let it dry fully and then iron each motif well on the reverse on a lowish heat. This will set the paint. You can also throw it in the dryer on a short spin. Voila, your custom tablecloth is ready to use!

5 To wash, ideally spot-clean if you can, but if you have set the paint with the iron, you can do a cool machine-wash and line-dry.

DIY Project #3

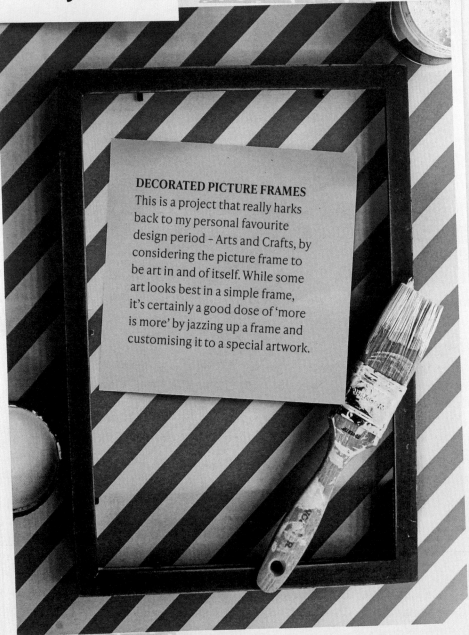

DECORATED PICTURE FRAMES
This is a project that really harks back to my personal favourite design period – Arts and Crafts, by considering the picture frame to be art in and of itself. While some art looks best in a simple frame, it's certainly a good dose of 'more is more' by jazzing up a frame and customising it to a special artwork.

YOU'LL NEED:
- ✳ A picture frame
- ✳ Primer
- ✳ Sample pots of paint in your chosen colours
- ✳ Clear varnish
- ✳ Paintbrushes
- ✳ Glass cleaner and cloth
- ✳ Drop cloth or newspaper

1 Choose a nice boxy style frame that has a good flat surface for painting your design on. Remove the backing and glass from the frame and set aside. Lay your frame on your drop cloth

2 Many frames have a lacquered or veneer type finish that doesn't hold paint super well, so unless your frame is raw timber, I recommend giving it a coat or two of primer and letting it dry.

3 Now it's the fun bit – start painting. Stripes or checks are a classic way to go and juxtapose nicely with a more painterly artwork. You could also look to more traditional folk and craft motifs for simple designs – geometrics or dots, flowers or squiggles. With frames for my own pieces, I have sometimes extended the artwork right out onto the frame.

4 Leave your frame to dry. Once completely dry, give it a coat of clear varnish – either with a brush (watch for drips) or use a spray. Let that dry.

5 Reassemble your frame and give the glass a good clean on both sides using glass cleaner and a lint-free cloth. Pop in your artwork, seal the frame back up and hang on your wall.

6 These types of frames look great in groups of three or more. Second-hand shops are a great source of base frames you can update – make a note on your phone of the sizes you need and take a measuring tape with you when you go hunting.

If at first you don't succeed, try and try again! I find it so empowering when I accomplish something I wasn't sure I could do and it makes me want to do more!

C141 **Dulux**

Devil's

Naena

Churc

C131 **Dulux**
COLOURS
NEW ZEALAND

Fort Street

Snells Beach

DIY Project #4

PAINTED PLANT POTS

I love turning boring pots into functional pieces of art. The texture of most plant pots is perfect for painting with regular wall paint.

✳ If I'm going to use them outdoors I use a primer first and seal with a top coat to make them last longer.

✳ Use masking tape to create geometric shapes or let your creativity run wild with beautiful organic lines and patterns.

✳ Paint markers are a great and easy way to add detail and patterns on top of painted shapes for indoor pots.

✳ You can also make simple stencils out of coated cardboard or paper (magazine covers or cereal boxes work well), use repositionable spray glue to hold them in place, and a sponge to apply paint.

My favourite shapes
to paint are bold
and organic –
keeping the pattern
loose and informal
means not having to
get the ruler out or
stay within the lines.

CHAPTER ELEVEN

Celeb-rating

I'm a sucker for a beautiful glass.
Nothing says 'celebrate' like
something bubbly in a pink coupe.

WELCOME TO THE VIBRANT WORLD OF CELEBRATIONS AND ENTERTAINING IN A MAXIMALIST HOME.

Where more is more and every gathering is an opportunity to dazzle and delight. I couldn't write this book and not include a picture of one (okay, maybe more than one) Christmas tree, because having an abundantly eclectic home is the most perfect backdrop for the memories we make.

This chapter is dedicated to those who believe in the power of excess, colour, and joy in creating unforgettable moments. From the sparkle of Christmas to the elegance of dinner parties, these are opportunities to share all the joy you've been creating in your home, with people you really like (hopefully), or at least want to show off a bit to. I can guarantee that you will be sending people home happy and bursting with inspiration for their own abode.

Entertaining

Maximalist entertaining is about embracing abundance in every aspect of your celebration. It is the art of layering textures, patterns and colours to create a rich, sensory experience for your guests. Here, we delve into the philosophy behind maximalist entertaining and how it translates into unforgettable gatherings that celebrate life's special moments.

Let's start with the humble (not for long!) dining table. Over the last few years, we have seen a return to the good ole home dinner party and I'm here for it. I don't think there is much more that shows friends and loved ones how much they mean to you than a shared meal in the heart of your home. Great food is a major part of it, but so is the tablescape. And for those of us that

Entertaining retro-style!
I love Australian homewares
brand Sage and Clare for
their colourful, bold textiles.

love a bit of indulgent décor, it's kind of the best part. And yes, it's so much more than just setting a table!

My lovely step-mother-in-law, Martine, a chic and extravagant French woman, is the queen of dinner parties – no occasion is too small for her to make it extra special. There's no such thing as a casual lunch in her book! Everything is considered, from the food to the table setting, to the way the napkins are folded – it makes you feel like it's a celebration. I'm under no delusion of the amount of work and planning that goes into this, but it's such a pure expression of love to her family and friends. The amount of 'oohs' and 'aahs' expressed throughout the course of an evening at my in-laws is quite funny. How wonderful to inspire such awe and delight with something as everyday as eating dinner. I've learned a lot from Martine, and she kindly keeps me stocked in tablecloths and vases from her travels.

You might not realise it, but you may already be a bit of a tablescaping pro. What is tablescaping? It is the art of setting the table, maximalist style. It came to the fore in 2020 when, unable to go out to restaurants, people started spending hours glamming up their at-home dining situations. Think outrageous tablecloths, mismatched vintage plates, colourful glassware, elaborate centrepieces, multicoloured candles, and a florist-load of flowers. Food is almost the afterthought.

It can be an easy thing to have a laugh at, the extent to which some people decorate their dining tables for the sake of their nearest and dearest (who are probably just very hungry), and for the 'Gram. But there's something incredibly romantic about going to such an effort. If you're partial to a bit of plate collecting or linen hoarding, it also serves as the

perfect creative outlet. I am unashamedly obsessed with how people set their tables and am always saving pictures and ideas for inspiration.

Tablescaping is a maximalist's dream. This is not the place for a plain linen tablecloth and a few sprigs of rosemary, oh no. You really want to cram in as many patterns and textures as you can. It needs to look like both tons of effort (it is) and yet also effortless, like you just happened to throw it all down and have it land in the most adorable, whimsical dinner party layout imaginable. Nothing should match too well – that shows far too much foresight and effort. Instead, everything should be a little mismatched, a little shabby, a lot loved.

A few years ago, interior trends and social media were all about the 'shelfie' – artfully arranged objects on a shelf, a pleasing corner of calm in perhaps an otherwise chaotic house. The tablescape is a more grown-up version, a grander declaration of style that also shouts 'I have friends', even if you don't. It's essentially an adult version of a doll's tea party, and who didn't love throwing those – no rude guests, minimal catering requirements.

My personal forays into tablescaping have had mixed results. A couple of years ago I had grand plans for Christmas tablescaping – hand-sewing eight metres of fringing on to a round tablecloth; collecting kitsch Christmas ornaments to mix amongst brightly coloured dried flowers; digging out vintage paisley print plates, with colourful glass bowls full of fancy wrapped sweets. It was glorious for about a day before it went up in flames, literally. I had seriously misjudged the burn time on some of

Tablescaping is a maximalist's dream. This is not the place for a plain linen tablecloth and a few sprigs of rosemary, oh no.

Get creative
with your
decorations
and take direct
inspiration
from the food
by including
ingredients.

Dinner parties are supposed to be
fun, so make them fun for yourself
by designing a menu and place
cards that match the meal.

my locally made candles and as I said goodbye to my friend at the door (she had come for a pre-event perv of my creation), I returned to the entire dining table up in flames. I don't have any photographic evidence of this as it was seconds before total disaster. Fortunately, I was fast enough with a bucket of water to save the table, but my tablecloth? Completely unsalvageable. Hours of work, quite literally up in smoke. It wasn't just the table that suffered; I managed to smash a hole in the wall with a broom while trying to turn off the smoke alarm. Minutes later my husband Sam walked in from work, saying, 'Mmm, what's cooking?' before taking in the scene in front of him: a soaking wet smouldering dining table, me with broom in hand, wild-eyed and in tears over my lost handiwork. Needless to say, the charred remains did not make it on to Instagram.

However, I'm not deterred from tablescaping. Like a phoenix rising from the ashes, I'm determined to keep styling my table with the most outrageous, Mad-Hatter-tea-party-esque settings I can muster. I might just settle for fewer candles next time. Tablescape responsibly and always check you have working smoke detectors!

The level of extravagance you want to go to is entirely dependent on what you feel like and what you're serving. For a friend's special birthday, you might want to go Marie Antoinette levels of frou-frou, with silk ribbons tied around champagne coupe stems. Or for a more relaxed dinner, keep it rustic and use fresh produce to dress the table.

Food

Ultimately your table wants to complement the food, and so the way you decorate will be reflected by the style of food and drink you are serving. Fresh, colourful summer salads lend themselves to light and bright materials and textures that evoke a feeling of warm weather and beachy days – rattan, stripes, an icy jug of something yum to drink are all great additions to a table like that. While perhaps for a hearty winter supper, you think the other way, with plaid, rich jewel tones, chunky pottery and pops of metallics to reflect the candlelight you'll be using.

Table Linen

The humble tablecloth really doesn't get enough credit for its ability to transform the kitchen/work-from-home desk/dumping ground into a beautiful dining space. Layering two fabrics is an easy way to add texture and interest as a base for your table. Lengths of fabric cut to size work just as well as any tablecloth and are a great way to get a custom look. I like to start with my larger piece covering the whole table and then an angled drape of my second cloth across the middle of the table – just make sure it is sitting flat so you can still put glasses on top!

I like to use placemats even when using a tablecloth – it adds a visual layer, saves your tablecloth (somewhat), and also makes guests feel more relaxed as it provides a place to leave cutlery, etcetera.

Cloth napkins are a must, unless you're hosting a large group. Like the tablecloth, they signify effort and that shows you care. To make it easier, at the end of dinner throw them in some hot water with detergent to soak; they will wash out easier, ready for next time. There are some super cute ways you can customise the humble napkin, by dying them to the perfect colour, adding a trim or a wavy edge, or even a little embroidery.

Tableware

Use what you have for plates and cutlery, you can tie the settings together using other styling elements. For example, if you have blue plates – just bring in some of that colour in the accessories you use to make them look intentional. Similarly, if you have mismatched pieces, make that part of your overall look.

Don't go buying a whole new dinner set (unless this is the perfect excuse you have been waiting for!). Collecting beautiful serving dishes, platters and jugs over time gives you options for occasions like this, and I love digging out something special to use. Think ahead about what you'll be serving and what dishes you will need. Pre-set the table before you start cooking so you avoid accidentally using pieces while cooking, like all the spoons.

Glassware

I'm not one for following the rules with glasses, and while sometimes I do wish I had the right glass for the particular type of wine, I love my colourful hand-blown tumblers too much not to use them. Most of mine are made by Matthew Hall Glass in Auckland, and when I first started collecting, I never used them. They sat pretty in a cabinet, then I started using them for special occasions, and now most of them are in daily rotation. I can honestly say that I get so much more joy from them now – even with the risk that one might get broken. It's worth it to drink out of something beautiful 'just because'.

Table Decorations

This all comes back to the style of the food you're serving, and matching that vibe. Get creative with your decorations and take direct inspiration from the food by including ingredients. There is a real trend at the moment for fresh fruit and vegetables as styling props – and why not? They're beautiful!

Keep it practical – everything should ideally be below head height to allow for conversation, and allow space to put down dishes and plates as needed. While a 'table centrepiece' tends to make you think of a single large arrangement, think of it as still life that is different, but lovely, from every angle around the table. A large arrangement can look amazing on the table before you all sit down, but lift it out of the way when you go to eat so everyone can see each other.

Fresh flowers are a must, but you'll find you need far less than you think when you keep it functional – use small posies or decorative herbs, and containers that don't take up too much space on the table. I love looking out for nice little jars, bottles and pots that are useful for this. Cool eateries are great for inspo for this sort of thing!

If you're feeling you need a bit extra or the occasion demands it, I love a handwritten menu and place cards.

Lighting

Lighting is key for setting a mood and creating a sense of relaxation. Move some lamps into the room and turn those overhead lights off! Candles are great but again, keep it simple and don't overdo it – you don't want to be moving lit candles when the food comes out. There are some great options for wireless USB-charged lights that can look great, and even better, they'll work outside too.

Fun

Most importantly, hosting a dinner party should be as fun and easy as possible, so make it what you want it to be! Use the good china, put on your favourite music and enjoy yourself – if you're having a good time, you can be sure everyone else will be too. For me, that means always serving food that I can prep

Paper lanterns are my favourite decoration – they fold flat to store but make such a big impact.

well ahead and pull out of the oven to serve. I also like to lean heavily on elements I don't need to cook but are a really delicious addition: a beautiful loaf of sourdough, good cheeses, fancy snacky things and great wine. Of course, these things are better with a story, and your local farmers' market is a treasure trove for picking up some of these yummy bits and pieces that will make your party unforgettable.

Christmas

One of my favourite things about Christmas is how we all do it so differently. I'm intrigued with how others celebrate and I'm forever stealing ideas and traditions to try myself – to varying levels of success. It all takes on a different form when you're the one who gets to make the magic (to varying levels of enthusiasm). I'm a bit of a Christmas chameleon – I frequently change it up depending on how inspired or energetic I'm feeling.

We don't have children in our home but that's fine, because as adults we're allowed a good dose of magic and whimsy too. Don't let anyone tell you otherwise!

Some years I have started early and gone hard on the festive decorations with up to four trees, each a different colour and with a different theme. Other years I have exhausted my festive mojo with commercial styling jobs long before December arrives and I'm left half-heartedly throwing a tree up the week before the big day. But no matter what, I love our tree(s) with all my heart and will still lie underneath gazing at the fairy lights long after I should be in bed.

New Zealand, and the southern hemisphere in general can be a bit of a funny spot for Christmas. Where on one hand we're decking the halls, we're also usually putting the outdoor furniture out on

the deck, complaining about how hot it is, while donning a paper Christmas hat. Having a summer Christmas was very high up on my list of concerns when we moved to New Zealand, but as with anything, you adapt and there are plenty of perks to go along with it. Large gatherings are much easier when you can spill out into the garden, or even better, meet at the beach or park for a picnic.

Our climate allows me to feel I have the freedom to make my festive theme anything I want (which of course you can wherever in the world you are, but there's something cosy about red and green on a dark winter's night), and I've run the gamut on this. Some years I've done a full tropical Christmas theme complete with faux flowers and paper cocktail umbrellas, while others I've opted for a more restrained decoration of only ribbons – just whatever takes my fancy that year.

I'm lucky in that I usually have a bundle of new Christmas decorations I've been sent to style prior to the big day, but I'm always increasingly conscious of reducing waste from Christmas and being mindful of what I purchase. My weakness is vintage glass baubles – the more patina on the surface, the better. Besides, it is the pieces with history that bring the most joy. I like tying together a bit of a colour scheme using hand-tied bows – the last few years have been the same black and white striped ones and I don't see myself tiring of them any time soon.

It's not all about the tree though; I want a home to feel festive from the moment I step through the front door. Scratch that – *before* I step through the door. I love a wreath – it might just be the most inviting thing ever. From there, I love touches of decorations wherever possible, a few festive additions to the sideboard, mantle and table.

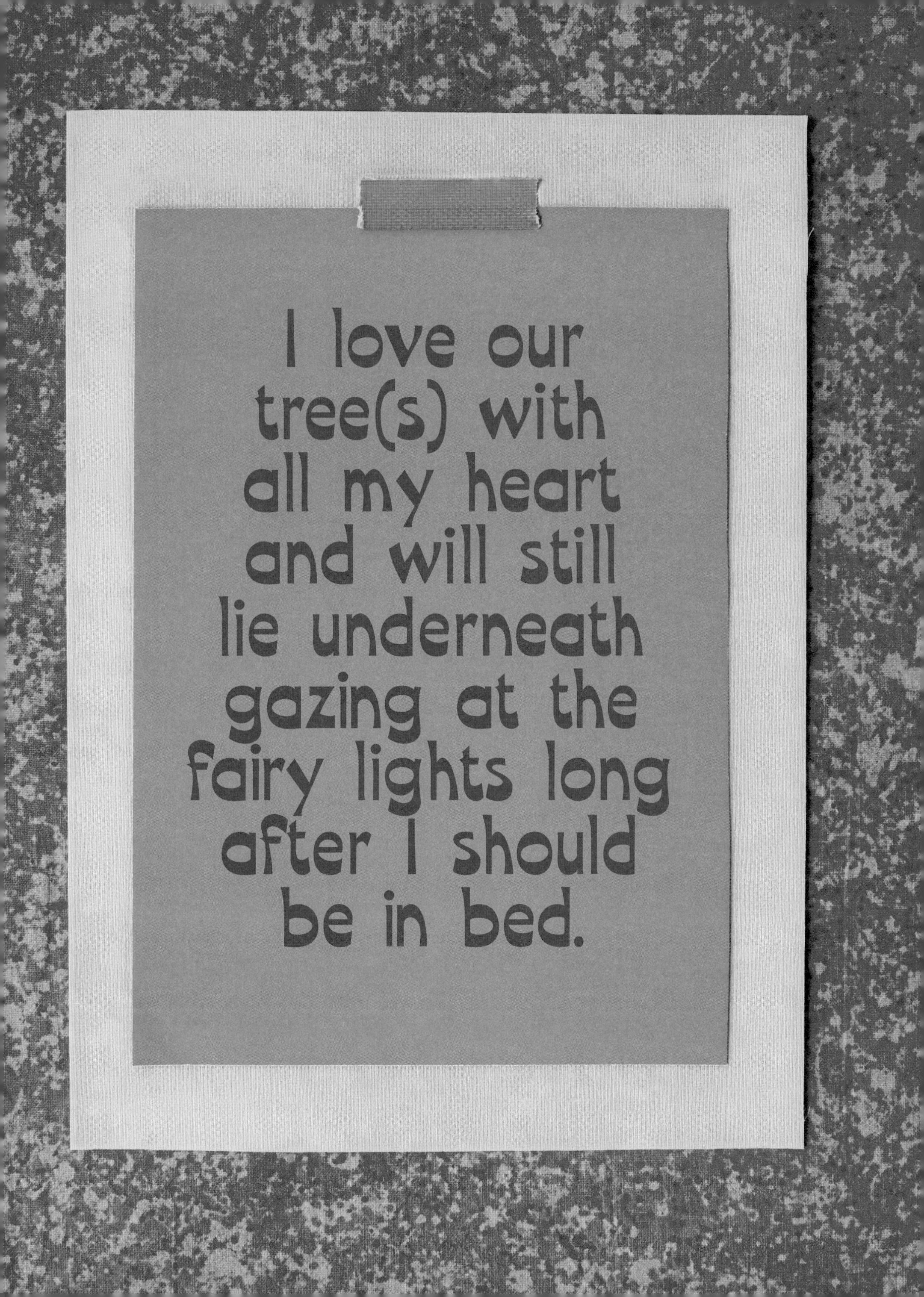

I love our
tree(s) with
all my heart
and will still
lie underneath
gazing at the
fairy lights long
after I should
be in bed.

If there is ever a time for abundance, Christmas is it. Let's say 'No' to sad beige Christmases and indulge our love for all things colourful, sparkly and more than a bit magical.

My English heart struggles with the empty hearth around Christmas, it just feels wrong – so I festoon our wood burner with colourful paper lanterns. If it's not needed for heat, it can be used as the scaffolding for extravagant Christmas joy!

Giftwrapping (not just at Christmas) is another place I love to sprinkle some magic, inspired mostly by people I know who wrap things so beautifully you feel special and loved without even needing to open the present. Fabric plays a big part in how I like to wrap, either wrapping gifts entirely in fabric squares (furoshiki) or by cutting or tearing my own ribbons from lovely fabrics and using them with paper wrap. I'm absolutely obsessed with ribbons and twines made from Indian fabric offcuts – the colours and patterns are so wonderful. I also love to make the wrapping part of the gift if I can, finding a vintage scarf perfect for the recipient and wrapping their main gift in that.

If there is ever a time for abundance, Christmas is it. Let's say 'No' to sad beige Christmases and indulge our love for all things colourful, sparkly and more than a bit magical.

Flowers

I love flowers but I don't grow my own (yet, anyway!), however my garden is still a treasure trove when it comes to creating my own floral displays – large and small. This has always been a trick of my mother's, to buy a bunch or two of inexpensive flowers and dramatically fill them out with leaves and branches from the garden. You can make a $20 bunch look like a much grander display, and it's also much less heartbreaking when they inevitably wilt a few days later. I'm under no delusion of being a florist and have such awe and admiration for those professionals – nothing can ever really beat an incredible arrangement by a skilled florist. But, as in styling anything, once you have an eye for colour, shape, scale and composition you really can trust yourself to put things together. Or even just have some fun playing around with it. And that's the really great thing about flowers – they can rarely look bad.

Just a touch of greenery can really make a difference to how your home feels. We have a thriving grapefruit tree in our back garden but neither of us can eat the fruit, however a cut branch with a couple of small fruit on them looks so beautiful in a vase or jug, or as part of a larger arrangement.

A friend of mine encouraged me to get myself a 'frog' – a weighted spiky disc that sits at the bottom of a vase or container, giving you much more control over the placement of your flowers. You stick them to a spike and it gives you a more open arrangement and also means you can use pots or jardinieres instead of just traditional vases. I love using mine, but I'm wanting to challenge myself to use it to create more sculptural displays.

It feels really good to use an antique vase I have picked up on my travels and give it new life (literally). Let the vessel inspire the arrangement. You'll find yourself stretching your creativity just by using a different style vase.

It's not
Christmas
at our place
without ...

Handmade ornaments ...

Giant paper lanterns ...

Handmade table
decorations ...

Trees (plural!) ...

Lots of bows and ribbon ...

Something old and
something new ...

Dogs in silly outfits ...

... and a bucket-load
of colour!

LOVE! Blues

CHAPTER TWELVE

Last but not least

SO WHAT'S NEXT FOR MY HOME (AND YOURS!)?

This book contains photos of my home over the last 10 years, and I'm not ashamed at how much it has changed (I mean, I *have* made a book about it!). I never think of 'finding my style' as some ultimate end goal, where I'll hang that last picture and contentedly sigh knowing that I'm 'done'. Design for me is ever evolving and it's as much about the process – the collecting, the making, the curating, even the painting – as it is about what it looks like. I find myself being swept up in trends, both from what I see in the world of interiors, and my own little rabbit holes and fascinations. I move from light to dark, from busy to calm(er), from more retro to modern, to more folk art to abstract, in waves. Rather than fight it I ride those waves; I look back on my past designs and ideas with fondness, even when they're not who I am now.

If I was to start entirely from scratch, I'd be sure to trust my gut. Knowing now, that if there isn't at least a little dose of nerves involved in a big design decision, that I'm playing it too safe. I wouldn't waste my time worrying about what other people think – they are people I don't really know, and would never actually be in my home. I'd dive right in much sooner and fast-forward to the state of play I now find myself at.

I don't know what our home will look like in the future, but I know it will be different. I know I'll look back at this book and see a moment in time; I'll see pieces I still use and love used in different ways. I'll see decisions I won't make again. But mostly, I'll see a home well loved and well lived. A canvas for ideas, self-confidence, and self-expression. Something I hope all of our homes can be.

And so my lovely maximalists...
I hope that MUCH has helped and inspired you to explore your own creativity within your home (and beyond!). In a world that is manufactured to have us conform, marching to the beat of your drum and having confidence in your own voice is a radical and beautiful thing.

If I can leave you with any last notes, it would simply be to do what you love and do it with conviction – a lot of it. Don't sweat making mistakes and don't give a hoot about what anyone else thinks. Lastly, just have loads of fun with it – a home should be a happy place. We need more of that.

A home for me has always been full of colour and possibilities; it's the place where we can most be ourselves – and, perhaps more importantly, the version of ourselves we most want to be ...

Resources

I'm all about finding inspiration anywhere and everywhere but here are a few of my tried-and-true spots online. Scribble down your favourites here too!

Websites I love for design inspiration
yellowtrace.com.au
thedesignfiles.net
architecturaldigest.com/clever
domino.com

YouTube
I'm a big fan of YouTube, both for nosing around amazing houses and learning how to do DIY. Some of my favourite channels for house-nosing are:

Quintessence
youtube.com/@quintessenceblg

House & Garden Design Notes
youtube.com/@HouseAndGardenMagazineUK

The Modern House
youtube.com/@themodernhouse_films

Architectural Digest
youtube.com/@Archdigest

Never Too Small
youtube.com/@nevertoosmall

Places to buy affordable art online
(Besides your local galleries of course!)

partnershipeditions.com
drool-art.com
printclublondon.com
jumbledonline.com
artfinder.com

And my personal favourites you'll have seen throughout this book
jennyojens.com
victoriatopping.com
fleurwoodsart.com

Artwork credits

All artwork/illustrations by Evie unless stated.
Front cover: Artwork on Samsung Frame TV is Gauguin; *Vinyl Guy* and *On Track* artworks by Jenny o Jens.
Back cover: Landscape by Evie Kemp; *Soul Dancing* by Victoria Topping.
P4/5: From left: Vintage neon sign; Dog artwork x 3 by Grace Helmer; Iris Apfel vase by Lovestar; *Look at this* (bum) postcard by David Shrigley; woman with parakeet by Sandra Eterovic; Wow postcard unknown.
P10: From left: Landscape by Evie Kemp; *Soul Dancing* by Victoria Topping; *Canny Grannies* by Victoria Topping.
P21: David Hockney portrait by Tom Bingham; Campbell's Soup poster by Andy Warhol from Te Papa; pink lady print from CSA Images.
P22: Clockwise from top left: *Sit Stay* by Evie Kemp; portrait by Evie Kemp; small artworks *Still Life with Lemons, Orange and a Rose* by Sarah Williams; *Vanitas with Violin and Glass Ball* by Sarah Williams; *Vinyl Guy* by Jenny o Jens; vintage scissors; *On Track* by Jenny o Jens; artwork on TV is by Toiletpaper.
P24: Pink dog artwork by John Bond; lamp sculpture by Moomi.
P25: POP! Prints by Playtype.
P28: *Large Fancy Room* framed tea towel by David Shrigley.
P31: Dog wall includes artworks by Tom Bingham, Evie May Adams, Colleen Pugh, Sophie Watson, Evie Kemp, Grace Helmer, Devon Smith, Odd One Out; Popcorn artworks by Madeleine Child; landscape painting unsigned.
P33: *On Track* artwork by Jenny o Jens; blue lady artwork by Quirky Bowerbird.
P34: Almost all artwork vintage – artwork on frame TV is *Two Hounds* by Jacopo Bassano.
P37: Lower left-hand artwork is a reproduction of a Picasso.
P38/39: Artworks by Evie Kemp (that's me).
P44: *Soul Sis* artwork by Fleur Woods.
P46/47: Selwyn Muru totem sculptures; ceramic totem sculpture by Helen Yau; *Soul Sis* artwork by Fleur Woods; *Head on Fire* print by Hester Finch on right-hand wall.

P54: Resin budgies by Pete Cromer; ostrich lamp by Abigail Ahern; matchbox print by Joanne Ho.

P56: *Heron Make-up Artist* by Hello Dodo; neon shapes by Nanolight; Iris Apfel vase by Lovestar.

P59: Flower artwork in dining room shot is by Jenny o Jens; butter dish by Studio Soph/Sophie Holt.

P62/63: Clockwise from left: Portrait by Evie Kemp; cat cushion by Klaus Haapaniemi; vintage postcard; antique Chinese cabinet; marble table and ceramic lamp (no reference); Marija Kori sofa section; vase from West Elm; gold cabinet by Paul Evans; rug by George Sowden; striped cushion unknown; yellow cabinet – Evie's.

P70: *Work Hard* print by Anthony Burrill; woman with parakeet by Sandra Eterovic; altered dog artwork by Evie Kemp; hairdresser dog by Grace Helmer.

P72: Poster *Grrrr* by Roy Lichtenstein from the Guggenheim Museum.

P73: Woman with parakeet by Sandra Eterovic.

P76: Headboard by Wink Design in Christchurch; pot painted by Evie.

P79: Bug artworks by Evie Kemp.

P81: Pink dog artwork by John Bond; other dog artworks by Grace Helmer, Odd One Out, Evie May Adams, Tom Bingham, Evie Kemp, Colleen Pugh, Sophie Watson; lobster artwork by Victoria Topping; *On Track* by Jenny & Jens Fotokonst.

P84: Artwork (in reflection) and wallpaper by Evie Kemp; custom resin handles by The Arc Dept; bathmat from Sage and Clare.

P87: Ligne Roset Togo chair in Pierre Frey fabric; artwork on Samsung Frame TV is Gauguin; *Vinyl Guy* and *On Track* artworks by Jenny & Jens Fotokonst.

P88: Still life by Jenny o Jens.

P90: Vintage Odense poster by Viggo Vagnby; pink dog by John Bond.

P91: Still life by Jenny o Jens.

P93: From left: Landscape by Evie Kemp; *Soul Dancing* by Victoria Topping; *Canny Grannies* by Victoria Topping.

P96: Bathmat from Sage and Clare.

P99: Ceramic sculpture by Helen Yau.

P103: Woman with parakeet by Sandra Eterovic.

P104: *Too Much* punch needle jacket by Evie Kemp.

P105: Chair artwork by Evie Kemp.

P111: *Sit Stay* by Evie Kemp.

P115: Poster *Grrrr* by Roy Lichtenstein from the Guggenheim Museum.

P116: Rug after Franz Marc Yellow Cow.

P120: Vintage coffee machine prints – unknown.

P122: *On Track* by Jenny & Jens Fotokonst.

P126: *Soul Dancing* by Victoria Topping; *Canny Grannies* by Victoria Topping.

P129: *Heron Make-up Artist* by Hello Dodo; second-hand neon – vintage; dog print by Grace Helmer; bug artworks by Evie Kemp; all art vintage and unknown except lower right-hand portrait by Evie Kemp.

P130: TV Artworks: *Caravaggio's Cat* by Marc Dennis; *Exhale* by Sheila Fuseini.

P133: From left: Landscape by Evie Kemp; *Soul Dancing* by Victoria Topping; *Canny Grannies* by Victoria Topping.

P137: Prints by Colin Vernon Wheeler and Albert Namatjira.

P138: Resin budgies by Pete Cromer; artwork on TV by Gauguin.

P140: Bowie artwork by Evie Kemp.

P143: Campbell's Soup poster by Andy Warhol from Te Papa; TV girl vintage poster in old TV frame – artist unknown.

P144: Vintage lady portraits, artists unknown; *Stardust* by Victoria Topping.

P148: *Green Lamp* by Evie Kemp.

P151: *Hide & Seek* by Evie Kemp.

P153: Pool artworks – largest one is of the Kaufmann House – artist unknown; top is a vintage motel illustration; right-hand two by Linda Tillman.

P154: From left to right: Vase painting by Evie Kemp; *Grapes and Lilies* print by Louise Henderson; still life in checkered frame by Evie Kemp; vintage pastel still life, artist unknown; large landscape, artist unknown.

P157: Towel on wall by ShopBando.

P158: *A Dinner Party With All The Wine*, *Dolly*, Exhibitionists & Eccentric *Debauchery* by Chloe Blades.

P159: *Electric Boots and Mohair Suits* by Evie Kemp.

P160: Pink dog by John Bond; zombie cat lampshade by Evie Kemp. Clockwise from top left: Sophie Watson; running lady – artist unknown; eyes – Kmart;

small dog by Sarah McNeil; pink handkerchief by the Guerrilla Girls; zombie Chihuahua by Alexandra Winthrop; David Bowie print by Chris Mousdale; *Beware of the Dog* by BT Livermore; portrait of Pebbles in blue frame by Devon Smith; *Wheel of Illustrator* by Sandra Eterovic; Elizabeth Taylor postcard – artist unknown; vintage Nat King Cole framed record; Bonnie dog portrait by Evie Kemp.

P162: Dog wall includes artworks by Tom Bingham, Evie May Adams, Colleen Pugh, Sophie Watson, Evie Kemp, Grace Helmer, Devon Smith, Odd One Out.

P164: Artwork on Samsung Frame TV is Gauguin; *Vinyl Guy* and *On Track* artworks by Jenny o Jens.

P167: Orange juice – vintage shop display piece; *My Life is Good* postcard by David Shrigley; *No, I do not have Flybuys* postcard by Anna Hoyle.

P168: Dog wall includes artworks by John Bond, Tom Bingham, Evie May Adams, Colleen Pugh, Sophie Watson, Evie Kemp, Grace Helmer, Devon Smith, Odd One Out.

P170/171: Artworks by Evie Kemp.

P174: Artwork on TV is La paresse by Félix Vallotton; ceramic poo by Bob Steiner for Bowel Cancer NZ.

P178: Image courtesy of Dulux NZ; artwork by Pop Shop Printables.

P181: Vintage artworks in bookcase; Poster *Grrrr* by Roy Lichtenstein from the Guggenheim Museum.

P185: *The Advantages of Being a Woman Artist* by the Guerrilla Girls; resin budgies by Pete Cromer; matchbox print by Joanne Ho; dog in a sweater artwork by Colleen Pugh; *Life is Fantastic* postcard by David Shrigley.

P186: Tray hung as art by iBride; landscape and table sculpture by Evie Kemp; blue vase in foreground by Lily Weeds; ceramic pot on books by Annie Smits Sandano.

P188: Artworks behind Evie – *Soul Dancing* and *Canny Grannies* by Victoria Topping; cut out vases by Lily Weeds (L) and Tāne Ceramics (R).

P191: Poster of work by Egon Schiele; vintage coffee machine print unknown.

P192: Dog art, mostly vintage; *Dog Show* poster by Odd One Out; a couple by Evie; *One for the Wolves* by Wolf Jaw Press.

P195: *Lobster* by Victoria Topping; lamp by Evie Kemp; bedhead by Wink design; quilt from Sage and Clare.

P201: *Mountain* by Jenny Palmer.

P204: Dog art – Sophie Watson, Odd One Out, Evie Kemp and vintage.

P210: *Vinyl Guy* by Jenny o Jens and vintage TV girl bought at a market.

P221: *Vinyl Guy* by Jenny o Jens.

P225: *Everything Happens* and *Say What You Feel* artworks by Tyler Spangler; *Influenced* by Evie Kemp.

P231: *Soul Sis* by Fleur Woods (corner of).

P235: *So Many Things to do* by Demii Whiffin.

P237: Vintage Odense poster by Viggo Vagnby; vintage coffee machine prints.

P240: *Soul Sis* by Fleur Woods.

P241: Vintage Odense poster by Viggo Vagnby; painted lampshades by Evie Kemp.

P244: Vintage Odense poster by Viggo Vagnby.

P247: Unsigned abstract artwork; table linens from Sage and Clare.

P248: Image credit: Yealands Photographer: Laura Court.

P252 *Head on Fire* by Hester Finch.

P254: Campbell's Soup poster by Andy Warhol from Te Papa.

P257: *Vinyl Guy* by Jenny o Jens; small print unknown; on TV unknown.

P262: Portrait by Evie Kemp; *So Many Things to do* by Demii Whiffin.

P269: *Growler* by Adam Cullen; Picasso print.

Every effort has been made to trace the owners for copyright material. The author and publisher welcome information leading to more complete acknowledgements in subsequent printing of the book and in the meantime extend their apologies for any omissions.

Thank you

This book is the culmination of years of work, passion and personal development. I don't think I truly appreciated how much has gone into it until I sat down to write these thank yous and realised this is over a decade of immense gratitude. I know I don't have space to cover all of this here, but please know my heart is bursting with it.

I'll start with my family, who have only ever encouraged being a bit of weirdo and taking your passions seriously but life less seriously. You are my home, always and forever.

My dear and darling friends who never falter in their support and are the most amazing cheer squad I could ever ask for. I'm sorry for all the emotional dumps and creative slumps that you always pull me up from – but you just make my brain work better. Thank you. Especially to Monique Doy, who took days to sit down with me and order my thoughts when I couldn't, and held me accountable. I did it!

A special thanks to my publisher, designer, creative powerhouse, and now friend, Tonia Shuttleworth – who has wrestled the tangled contents of my mind and archives into such a beautiful thing.

Thank you to my wonderful editors Lucinda Diack and Belinda O'Keefe who sympathetically and kindly tightened up my words, for which this book is much improved. And to Adrienne Pitts for the fun portraits of me, you're a delight, my joy in these is genuine.

To my agent Kimberly Singh and her fabulous sidekick Alex Quensell at Liquorice, who work so hard for me and take so much admin off my plate that frees me to create. Always in my corner, please don't leave me.

To all the artists and designers who inspire me daily, and many I'm lucky enough to call my friends. Without this creative community beside me I'd never have been able to pursue this wonderful journey of creativity. Looking around my home to see art and items made by magic hands is such a gift.

My collaborators and patrons that enable me to live and breathe design, I'm so grateful to you for continuing to support my creative endeavours and push me in to new and exciting things. Especially to the team at Dulux NZ, Davina Harper and Louise McKenzie-Smith who have had my back since I was just a wee pup – your influence and belief in me has been huge.

Lastly, my husband Sam, quite literally my better half – for every project you see within these pages has a patient (mostly), kind and extremely handy man behind the scenes and I couldn't (and wouldn't want to) do it without you.

Evie x

KOA PRESS

Published in 2024 by Koa Press Limited.
www.koapress.co.nz
@koapress

Much
ISBN 978-0-473-69952-9

10 9 8 7 6 5 4 3 2 1

Publisher and Director: Tonia Shuttleworth
Editor: Lucinda Diack
Proofreader: Belinda O'Keefe
Designer: Tonia Shuttleworth
Photographers: Evie Kemp @eviekemp,
Adrienne Pitts @hellopoe (pages 4–5, 9, 10, 22, 40, 50, 103, 126,
188, 265 & back cover) & Tonia Shuttleworth @toniashuttleworth.
Vector shapes: istock.com

A catalogue record of this book is available from the
National Library of New Zealand.

Printed in China by 1010 Printing.